Computational Intelligence in Business Analytics

Computational Intelligence in Business Analytics

Concepts, Methods, and Tools for Big Data Applications

Les Sztandera, Ph.D.,
Professor, Computer Information Systems,
School of Business Administration,
Kanbar College of Design,
Engineering and Commerce,
Philadelphia University

Associate Publisher: Amy Neidlinger
Executive Editor: Jeanne Glasser Levine
Operations Specialist: Jodi Kemper
Cover Designer: Alan Clements
Managing Editor: Kristy Hart
Project Editor: Elaine Wiley
Copy Editor: Bart Reed
Proofreader: Debbie Williams
Indexer: Lisa Stumpf
Compositor: Nonie Ratcliff
Manufacturing Buyer: Dan Uhrig

Upper Saddle River, New Jersey 07458

For information about buying this title in bulk quantities, or for special sales opportunities (which may include electronic versions; custom cover designs; and content particular to your business, training goals, marketing focus, or branding interests), please contact our corporate sales department at corpsales@pearsoned.com or (800) 382-3419.

For government sales inquiries, please contact governmentsales@pearsoned.com.

For questions about sales outside the U.S., please contact international@pearsoned.com.

Printed in the United States of America

First Printing June 2014

ISBN-10: 0-13-355208-X
ISBN-13: 978-0-13-355208-9

Pearson Education LTD.
Pearson Education Australia PTY, Limited.
Pearson Education Singapore, Pte. Ltd.
Pearson Education Asia, Ltd.
Pearson Education Canada, Ltd.
Pearson Educación de Mexico, S.A. de C.V.
Pearson Education—Japan
Pearson Education Malaysia, Pte. Ltd.

Library of Congress Control Number: 2014934908

*To my family for their unfailing support,
without whose help my passion for computational
intelligence would not have been fully realized.*

Contents

Foreword

"In God we trust. Everyone else bring data."
—W. Edwards Demming

We are at the dawn of a new era. An era that almost crashed and died quietly without many people noticing or paying attention. This era of computational intelligence is about to make all of the accomplishments by the baby boomers obsolete. In this era, computational intelligence paradigms will be embedded into everything—your credit card, the train tracks, the books you read, the stores you frequent, your body! This era will cause massive disruption in businesses throughout the globe. This is an era where new business empires have rapidly emerged—the likes of Google, Facebook, and LinkedIn—and this will be an era where industry giants who are not forward thinking go by the wayside. But by far, a bulk of the industry giants around the globe are in a race to figure out how to capitalize on this maturing technology—to make their businesses not just survive but thrive. They strive to make their businesses "frictionless"—to relentlessly pursue excellence while we are sleeping, to automatically adjust to the ever-changing world without human intervention and delays, and to take into account complexities that our marvelous brain takes into account automatically, but when we try to articulate these complexities we get lost in the process.

Computational intelligence has its roots in artificial intelligence (AI), which started very humbly at Dartmouth College in 1956. In the 60s, artificial intelligence research was well funded in both the United States and United Kingdom. However, by the mid-70s, much of the early excitement and promise of AI had evaporated. Once again in the early 80s, commercial enterprises started investing in research and a new generation of "expert systems" appeared, creating a billion-dollar market. However, by the late 80s the rigidity of those rules-based systems faded into obscurity. Very quietly in the 90s, AI gained new momentum via a foothold in supply chain and logistics, which was being swept up as part of the business process reengineering projects that spanned the globe in an attempt to drive process efficiency and cost savings. The complexities of supply chains with hundreds and thousands of customers, plants, suppliers, and modes of transportation proved to be a very good proving ground for the highly evolved optimization techniques honed through decades of AI research.

From that early launch pad, AI shed its moniker and has taken on many new names—predictive analytics, data mining, advanced analytics, simulation, optimization, just to name a few—to distance itself from the failed promises. From this new vantage, computational intelligence has emerged to deliver concrete results and value for businesses—just as supply chain and logistics optimization did in the early 90s. Many of these early successes have been kept as "trade secrets" by businesses around the globe. Today, after more than 50 years of starts and fits, computational intelligence is ready to deliver on the initial promises of artificial intelligence through a whole new generation of savvy business managers and technologists.

As many of the innovative business executives who made the decision to keep the early computational projects a trade secret know, this technology can deliver amazing business value—business value that can create a *sustainable* competitive differentiation, which is much easier to aspire to but much harder to attain. While the early projects required a lot of validation—because oftentimes the results were so massive that they defied all common wisdom—the new generations—the X-ers, the Millennials, and soon-to-be the Z-ers—trust and believe their technology much more than their own (or anyone else's) intuitions. This new wave of data scientists, leaders, managers, and consumers expect the computer to deal with complexities and make optimal decisions every time. They won't settle for anything less.

This book is the indispensable guide for those of you not familiar with the technology—whether you're a Boomer or part of the new wave. In this book, you'll learn the essence of the technology and understand how to apply it to practical real-world problems. Many of the examples cited contain transferable lessons to many other industries and problems. Embrace the examples and figure out how to make them work in your business and how to improve upon them so they create further value for your business. Then rinse and repeat until you've fully embedded this new wave into the very fabric of your business. That's how you get and keep sustainable competitive differentiation in this new era.

Michele Chambers
Chief Strategy Officer, Revolution Analytics

Acknowledgments

I would like to express my appreciation to Dr. Stephen Spinelli, Jr., for his vision to transform higher education. Under his leadership, Philadelphia University has become the model for professional university education. As part of the University's bold Strategic Plan, Dr. Spinelli led the way in formalizing the University's signature approach to teaching and learning, Nexus Learning, and establishing the unique College of Design, Engineering and Commerce, which is underpinned by an innovative curriculum based on trans-disciplinary, active, and real-world learning that is infused with the liberal arts—one where data analytics play a crucial role in academic discovery.

About the Author

Dr. Les Sztandera is Professor of Computer Information Systems in the School of Business Administration at Philadelphia University Kanbar College of Design, Engineering and Commerce. His research interests include data analytics and computational intelligence. He received his Doctor of Philosophy degree from the University of Toledo, Ohio, and his Master of Science from the University of Missouri. Dr. Sztandera has taught undergraduate and master's level courses as well as doctoral seminars in computational intelligence for more than 20 years. He was a recipient of the highest and the most prestigious appointment in the U.S. Fulbright Scholars program in 2003, and served as Fulbright Distinguished Chair at the School of Business and Economics (ISEG) in Lisbon, Portugal, teaching in the MBA and Ph.D. programs there.

Currently, Dr. Sztandera is teaching innovation MBA program courses in Technical Competitive Intelligence and New Product Development, as well as being involved in multidisciplinary industry-sponsored research projects as part of the new curriculum that draws on Philadelphia University's rich history in innovation and design, and long tradition of excellence in teaching and researching integrated product development. The curriculum meets the emerging needs of industry to educate managers, industrial designers, and engineers into more accomplished practitioners in the global product development processes.

Dr. Sztandera draws on his experience in the design and delivery of innovative curricula to facilitate crafting of cross-disciplinary projects. His cross-disciplinary work in encouraging the inclusion of computational intelligence principles and competences in undergraduate education led to the National Science Foundation grant award for Philadelphia University through the Division of Undergraduate Education in 1996. Since joining Philadelphia University in 1993,

Dr. Sztandera has been involved in a number of course and curricula developments. He proposed a sequence of courses coupled with laboratory assignments in which students worked on real-life problems. In 2004 he was instrumental in developing a Business Plus program for entering freshmen.

Complementary with his teaching effort, Dr. Sztandera has been involved in a variety of research activities in the field of computational intelligence. His research was funded by the U.S. Department of Defense, U.S. Department of Commerce, National Science Foundation, State Supercomputer Centers, and the American Heart Association, among others. Dr. Sztandera is an eminent scholar, and has a significant publication and teaching record. He has delivered papers, seminars, and workshops, and has published extensively on computational intelligence issues, as well as served as a Chair of International Conferences in the field.

1

Overview

Learning Objectives

- To know how to define data analytics
- To understand the function and uses of data analytics
- To demonstrate an understanding of current theory and research avenues in data analytics
- To understand why computational intelligence occupies a place in big data analytics
- To appreciate areas of ethical sensitivity in data analytics

1.1 Introduction

This book aims to help organizations gain a competitive edge in the marketplace through harnessing the power of computational intelligence approaches. Those approaches—fuzzy sets, artificial neural networks, and genetic algorithms—are at the core of every innovative business, from large corporations to small companies. Businesses that do not leverage computational intelligence will be quickly outperformed by those that do.

The chapters are designed to provide a foundation upon which one can differentiate one's business through computational intelligence approaches. Thus, the book provides the reader with guidance on how to create acceptable models in a relatively short period of time, and how to arrive at the right innovative decisions before the competition does.

The primary purpose of this book is to facilitate education in the resurgent computational intelligence areas of artificial neural networks, fuzzy sets, and genetic algorithms. The book is written as a text for a course at the graduate or upper-division undergraduate level. It could also be used for short intensive courses of continuing and executive education or as a self-study. No previous knowledge of computational intelligence tools is required to understand the material in this text.

Whereas most (if not all) literature on the topic utilizes statistical software packages, this book urges managers to take advantage of computational intelligence for analysis, exploration, and knowledge generation. As a result, readers are provided with the needed guidance to understand, model, discover, and interpret new patterns and new knowledge from historical evidence and large data sets, and become adept at building powerful models for prediction and classification that do not rely on statistics.

A process based on the exploration of business data with an emphasis on statistical and/or computational intelligence analysis is called Business Analytics. It is used by innovative companies committed to data-driven decision making to gain insights that inform business decisions, and down the road it can be used to automate and optimize business processes. Data obtained through Business Analytics are treated as corporate assets (added value) and are leveraged to gain a competitive edge.

The outcome of Business Analytics depends on data quality (to avoid junk in, junk out), entrepreneurial business analysts who understand the analysis and the business itself, as well as an organizational commitment to data-driven decision making. It should be stressed that entrepreneurial and skillful business analysts are at the core of obtaining competitive advantage for the business. They should operate at every level of their organizations instead of being an elite group of data scientists reporting directly to the executive suite. Those business analysts make the discovered insights actionable, as they discover new knowledge and utilize predictive power of computational intelligence approaches.

Business Analytics itself is used for the following purposes:

- To explore data to find new patterns and relationships (data mining)
- To evaluate and test previous decisions (randomized controlled experiments, multivariate testing)
- To explain why a certain outcome happened (statistical analysis, descriptive analysis)
- To venture into the future (forecast) results (predictive modeling, predictive analytics)

Once the business goal(s) of the analysis is agreed upon, an analysis methodology is selected and data are acquired to support the analysis. Data acquisition often involves extraction from many sources and business systems, data cleaning, dimensionality reduction, feature evaluation, and subsequent integration into a single repository, such as a data mart or a larger data warehouse. Competitive intelligence utilizing intelligent software agents might be used to locate and extract some of the needed data. The analysis is typically performed against a smaller sample set of data to verify its applicability first, and then used on all historical evidence the business has accumulated.

Analytic tools range from spreadsheets with statistical functions to complex data mining and predictive modeling applications. As patterns and relationships in the data are discovered, new questions are asked, new queries are sent, and the analytic process iterates until the business goal is met. This could be optimized by additional technologies such as optimization and/or genetic algorithms.

Deployment of predictive models involves ranking data and information, evaluating their "novelty indexes," and using the ranks to optimize real-time decisions within applications and business processes. One can also utilize Business Analytics at the tactical level of a business pyramid to tackle unforeseen events, and in many cases the decision making could be automated to support real-time inputs. It is its predictive power that makes computational intelligence insights actionable. The finding associated with an action that is deemed reliable, based upon past data, gives the decision maker a high degree of confidence.

Each chapter in this book is followed by a set of exercises, which are intended to enhance the understanding of the material presented in the chapter. The solutions to a selected subset of these exercises are provided in the instructor's manual, which also contains further suggestions for use of the text under various circumstances. The exercises are of varying levels of difficulty. The following rating system is applied to approximately indicate the amount of effort required for solving the exercises:

- **[Level 1]**—Problems at Level 1 are solvable within a day. They test the comprehension and mastery of fundamental concepts. If they relate to the use of software or writing computer code, the programming time is short.
- **[Level 2]**—Solving problems at Level 2 can take days or weeks (e.g., proof of concept programming or implementation). The chapters provide all the information necessary for solving Level 1 and Level 2 problems.

- **[Level 3]**—Problems at Level 3 are even harder, and their solutions can take several weeks or even months (e.g., semester-long projects). Many of these exercises are related to innovative avenues of current research.
- **[Level 4]**—Problems at Level 4 concern open research questions and could be topics of graduate theses or dissertations. Solving Level 3 and Level 4 exercises typically requires doing further literature searches and/or conducting extensive experiments.

It is recommended that the reader do the Level 1 and Level 2 exercises, and tackle at least some of the problems at Levels 3 and 4. Carefully working through Level 1 and Level 2 problems will reward the reader with a thorough understanding of the material of the chapters, and solving Level 3 and Level 4 exercises could turn a reader into an innovator!

1.2 A Need for Computational Intelligence in Business Analytics

There exists a need for a resource that can be drawn upon by an innovative organization that seeks to gain a competitive edge in the marketplace through harnessing the power of computational intelligence approaches. This book provides managers with the tools, knowledge, and strategies to differentiate their business and to successfully add value to their organization. The driving force behind this differentiation lies in utilization of computational intelligence approaches, such as fuzzy sets, artificial neural networks, and genetic algorithms. Those approaches are much more adequate for dealing with uncertainty and the complexity of today's organizations than the statistical analysis and tools currently utilized.

1.3. Differentiating Your Business Through Computational Intelligence

This book aims to provide a thorough introduction to the main issues associated with the design and implementation of computational intelligence tools that could add value to an organization.

In general, computer systems are not good at knowing what to do: every action the system performs must be explicitly anticipated, planned for, and coded by the programmers. If a computer system encounters a situation that its programmers did not anticipate, then the situation usually results in a system crash. For the most part, business managers accept that computers satisfy a purely computing (number crunching) role. For many applications (such as payroll processing), it is entirely acceptable. However, for an increasingly large number of business processes, managers require computer systems that could decide for themselves what they need to do in order to satisfy both their design objectives and tackle a given business problem. Such computer systems utilize computational intelligence tools. They must operate robustly in rapidly changing and often unpredictable environments. Thus, to some extent, these computer systems are *anthropomorphic* and utilize the power of computational intelligence techniques, such as fuzzy sets, artificial neural networks, and genetic algorithms.

The techniques are outlined in the book, and examples for suggested implementations are provided. It should be noted that these approaches are much more adequate for dealing with multiple data (both structured and unstructured) as well as with uncertainty and the complexity of today's organizations than the statistical analysis and tools most commonly used. Computational intelligence tools provide actionable insights for decision making in addition to their capability to explain the past.

For example, these tools (fuzzy sets, artificial neural networks, and genetic algorithms) could address problems and tackle tasks of product mechanical design within a framework of integrated design. The mechanical design process is usually divided in several subproblems from engineering and programming points of view. The fuzzy sets approach allows for the comparison of different stakeholders' points of view to one another and the final solution through a global compromise. This approach allows the mechanical design to be distributed in parallel tasks. The genetic algorithms and artificial neural networks tools could be used in order to encapsulate the data and analysis of each engineering design point of view. So, they allow for multiple constraints (factors of materials selection, reliability, performance, safety, and environmental impacts) to be incorporated into the mechanical design. Genetic algorithms and artificial neural networks also allow for exploration of new mechanical design solutions, thus fostering innovation.

Even more autonomous behavior of computer systems utilizing computational intelligence tools is expected in scientific applications. For example, when a space probe makes its long flight from Earth to outer planets in the solar system and beyond, a large ground crew of scientists is usually required to continually track its progress and decide how to deal with unexpected eventualities. This is not practical and very costly. For these reasons, organizations like the National Aeronautics and Space Administration (NASA) have been experimenting with making space probes more autonomous—giving them richer decision making capabilities and responsibilities, in part by utilizing computational intelligence tools.

Computational intelligence poses both a challenge and an opportunity for many businesses and organizations, and data scientists and researchers are at the forefront of learning how to leverage these changes for business impact.

I hope you enjoy learning about computational intelligence and its tools and how the industry is adapting to today's environment.

Exercises

1. [Level 1] Business internal databases are repositories of data and information gathered by a company, typically during the course of business transactions. They could be augmented by external, secondary data sources. Companies gather information about customers when they purchase a product, inquire about a service, or have a product serviced. Business internal databases are used by the companies to strengthen their relationships with customers and for direct marketing. Those databases could become quite large over time, and dealing with the vast quantity of data poses quite a challenge for decision makers. The managers are often further hindered by the relational nature of a database.

   Computational intelligence software helps managers make sense of the enormous mass of information contained in non-relational data warehouses. The software is capable of creating new knowledge that is actionable for decision makers, as it does not just have the ability to explain the past, but also possesses predictive power. Micromarketing refers to using a differentiated marketing mix for specific customer segments, sometimes fine-tuned for the individual shopper. Data analytics make micromarketing drive sales and business profits.

   Like many businesses nowadays, Target has utilized data analytics to micromarket—that is, to target each consumer with promotional materials designated for that individual. *The New York Times* reported on those practices on February 16, 2012 [Duhigg, 2012]. According to the report, titled "How Companies Learn Your Secrets," Target collects data on every person who shops at its department stores, assigning a unique code known as customer ID. If the consumer uses a credit card or coupon, fills out a survey, mails in a refund form, calls the customer center, or opens an e-mail, Target links those interactions with the customer ID. The company also collects demographic information, such as age, gender, ZIP Code, marital status, number of children, place of residence, and income, and has the ability to purchase additional data. Like many other innovative businesses, Target utilizes data analytics in its marketing research. One avenue of these analyses is to relate to the customers during major life events, such as having a baby, graduating from college, moving from state to state (or coast to coast), and so on.

How does Target identify specific customer segments, such as pregnant female consumers, for example? Target data scientists use the store's baby registry to identify consumers who have used it, and then backtrack to find out what products they had bought early in their pregnancy. The researchers discovered unique patterns that became clusters, and subsequently classes of consumers, and associated them with products. It appeared that women in their first 20 weeks of pregnancy purchased supplements such as calcium, magnesium, and zinc, and subsequently bought a lot of unscented lotions in their second trimester. In their third trimester, they purchased washcloths, hand sanitizers, soap, and cotton balls. Overall, Target data scientists identified 25 products, and came up with a "Pregnancy Prediction Score." This is just one of the metrics Target uses. It applies those metrics to all customers, and those who score high enough are contacted. In this particular "Pregnancy Prediction Score" case, the high-scoring customers are assumed to be pregnant, and receive targeted promotions on products Target predicts they will need. Reportedly, Target sales on mom-to-be and baby products have increased since the data analytics tools were applied.

Similarly, many of the company's online customers' data browsing habits are collected and analyzed. Do you think these data analytics practices are ethical?

1.1. [Level 1] Provide documented examples of data analytics usage by businesses. How many of these companies gained a competitive edge in the marketplace through harnessing the power of computational intelligence approaches?

2. If you do an Internet search on the phrase "faith-based businesses," the results direct you to companies that pursue a religious agenda. But, according to Fast Company [Safian, 2014], there is another kind of faith in business nowadays: the belief that a product or service can perform a radical industry makeover, completely change consumer habits, challenge economic assumptions, and enable city, county, and state officials to be proactive about health care, weather, and traffic emergencies.

With $452 million distributed in 2013, Bloomberg Philanthropies is among the largest philanthropic foundations in the United States. It differentiates itself by utilizing innovative and sophisticated data-driven solutions in its business processes. As a result, the foundation has been extraordinarily effective, as it positions itself for maximum impact [Safian, 2014].

2.1. [Level 2] Examine the data analytics tools used by Bloomberg and write a comprehensive report on them. Identify avenues of possible use of computational intelligence to further Bloomberg's philanthropic pursuits.

3. Fierce competition, time-to-market pressure, and an increasing demand for product differentiation call for more sophisticated, yet rapid product design. Businesses are increasingly seeking more efficient ways to integrate consumers' preferences into the product design process. Taking advantage of techniques from the field of computational intelligence, it is possible to construct systems that can computationally design products with specified desirable consumer characteristics.

3.1. [Level 3] Conduct research on techniques from the field of computational intelligence that deal with optimal design of products. Write a case study to illustrate the application of the computational intelligence approaches in your industry.

3.2. [Level 4] Propose a research project for your Ph.D. dissertation that will support the construction and deployment of a sophisticated, computational intelligence model to design products that your business unit is involved with.

2

Computational Intelligence Foundations

Learning Objectives

- To get acquainted with computational intelligence foundations
- To understand basic concepts and terms of artificial neural networks
- To understand fuzzy sets definitions, as well as research techniques and procedures for gathering, recording, analyzing, and reporting data with uncertainty constraints
- To get acquainted with neuro-fuzzy research tools for identifying business opportunities and/or solving business and science problems
- To understand basic concepts and terms of genetic algorithms
- To discover innovative and actionable insights that could be derived from the application of fuzzy sets (sets with boundaries that are not precise), artificial neural networks (universal approximators), and genetic algorithms (optimizers)

2.1 Introduction

Although analytical methods are applicable to problems involving a limited number of variables that are related to each other in a predictable way, the applicability of statistical approaches has just the opposite characteristics: They involve big data with a very large number of variables and a high degree of randomness. Even though these two approaches complement each other, they reflect the two extreme ends of complexity and randomness encountered in life. Therefore, their applicability is limited—and down the road, so is the ability to act upon them and make decisions based on their outcomes. Most problems, however, can be encountered between, or even outside, these two frameworks. They involve nonlinear systems with a very large number of attributes and complex interactions among the components, which are usually nondeterministic, but not as a result of randomness that could be captured by meaningful statistics. That raises a question: How do we deal with systems and their associated problems whose complexities are beyond those limits?

In general, we tackle problems in terms of systems that either model some aspects of reality or model a desired outcome—whether it is an object or a process. The purpose of constructing models to understand some phenomenon of reality is for learning how to control the phenomenon in a desirable way, making adequate predictions, and subsequently utilizing these capabilities for decision making. The purpose of modeling an object or a process is to obtain steps by which it can be constructed in such a way that desirable objective criteria are satisfied within given constraints.

In constructing a model, we always aim at maximizing its usefulness for decision making. This goal is always an outcome of an interaction between three key characteristics of every system model: complexity, reliability, and uncertainty. Those interactions are not yet fully understood. It seems that uncertainty plays a crucial role in constructing and executing a model. Usually, allowing for more uncertainty reduces complexity and increases the reliability of the resultant model. Therefore, uncertainty is an important aspect that could produce significant gains and more accurate models.

That is where computational intelligence has an upper hand. Its tools—fuzzy sets (sets with boundaries that are not precise), artificial neural networks (universal approximators), genetic algorithms (optimizers), as well as hybrid neuro-fuzzy systems—are capable of dealing with uncertainty much better than statistical approaches that can only represent randomness. They allow decision makers to discover innovative and actionable insights. Those tools are explained in the following sections.

2.2 Artificial Neural Networks

Artificial neural networks consist of numerous, simple processing units and weighted connections between them that can be trained to solve a given mapping problem. They can be programmed to store and then retrieve patterns, or to estimate sampled functions when we do not know the form of these functions. This, however, can be accomplished only within a specified framework, which is discussed next. Assuming that all x_i of the input signals and all y_j of the output signals belong to the interval [0,1], then $Y = f(X)$ with $Y \in [0,1]^n$, $X \in [0,1]^m$, and function f is continuous and represents the network [Hayashi et. al., 1992].

Supervised feed-forward neural networks can learn new patterns and recall old patterns [Anderson, 1983; Rumelhart et. al., 1986]. They can learn far more input-output relations than the number of neurons and synapses in the network architecture. Because neural networks do not use a mathematical model of how a system's output depends on its input, they are model-free estimators. Therefore, it is possible to apply the same neural network architecture to a variety of problems.

Artificial neural networks store function information using distributed encoding [Rumelhart et. al., 1986] by superimposing pattern information on the weighted connections between neurons. Distributed encoding enables neural networks to correctly operate on noisy patterns. It also enables neural networks to estimate continuous functions. In other words, neural networks are endowed with fault tolerance and graceful degradation. Distributed encoding causes cross-examination between stored patterns [Kosko, 1992; Rumelhart et. al., 1986]—that is, similar patterns tend to group together and new, large patterns may eliminate older, previously learned patterns. This limits the neural network's capacity [Rumelhart et. al., 1986]. Different learning schemes result in different storage capacities. Storage capacity ultimately depends on the number of neurons in a network and the connections between them [Anderson, 1983].

Biological neurons and synapses motivated the artificial neural network's topologies and dynamics [Anderson, 1983]. Artificial neurons are interpreted as simple input-output functions, such as threshold switches for two-state neurons and as asymptotic threshold switches for continuous neurons. Synapses are interpreted as adjustable weights. Overall, a neural network behaves like an adaptive function estimator.

In unsupervised artificial neural networks, the network architecture forms its own classification of patterns. The classification is based on common features in input patterns that are identified during the learning process.

The four primary artificial neural network topologies are Perceptron, Hopfield, Back-Propagation, and Kohonen [Galushkin, 2007]. They are being primarily used for characterization, association, classification and prediction, clustering, outlier analysis, as well as trend analysis.

Thus far, artificial neural networks have been successfully used for the following applications (among others):

- **Stock market analysis and selecting profitable stocks**—The analysis is based on historical evidence (that is, sets of samples), economic and other external conditions (which are often ignored in statistical approaches), and subsequent discovery and tracing of nonlinear patterns in order to approximate the underlying relationships and their weighted importance.
- **Hedge funds predictions**—Investors have long sought to improve the efficiency of modeling financial returns' volatility as a means by which to maximize directional trading returns from identifiable trading rules. Hedge Fund Trader [Ward-Systems, 2014] has helped many businesses gain a competitive edge through the employment of predictive capabilities of the Neuro Shell Trader.
- **Evaluating customer credit**—Credit scoring and evaluation are the key analytical techniques in credit risk evaluation, which has been an active research area in financial risk management. Artificial neural networks and their emotional models [Khashman, 2011] have been considered to be accurate tools for credit analysis.
- **Detecting fraudulent (inflated or false) claims**—Several elements are essential to carrying out the successful deployment of a fraud detection system. Historical evidence (past transactions) must be available to derive predictive outputs. The fraud events themselves and their relationships to specific transactions must be accurately defined. Profiles of the past behavior of both regular clients and fraudsters must be built into the model.
- **Forecasting sales**—Forecasting sales is an essential part of supply chain management, and is required to sustain profitability. A good sales-forecasting model is the one that takes into account all the factors affecting it. Apparel sales are affected by both exogenous factors such as size, price, color, climatic data, price changes, marketing strategies, and endogenous factors

like time. Although traditional statistical forecasting models are very popular, they model sales only on previous sales data and tend to be linear in nature. Artificial neural networks can efficiently model sales, taking into account both exogenous and endogenous factors, and allow for nonlinear approximation functions derived (learned) directly from the data [Frank et. al., 2003].

- **Identifying new customers**—Many innovative businesses have employed artificial neural network algorithms to identify specific prospective customers. This activity of identifying prospects and quantifying their likelihood to engage with the business has created a competitive advantage for many companies.
- **Image processing and pattern recognition**—This is an area of active current research, involving development of more sophisticated algorithms that can better deal with 3D object identification, especially in medical and surveillance applications.
- **Discovering new drugs and chemical structures**—Artificial neural networks have played significantly in aiding successful drug candidate identification and design. They have ensured that drugs make it to the market quicker with higher hit rates and earlier indications of human toxicity issues.

2.3 Fuzzy Sets and Systems

2.3.1 Introduction

Randomness is not the only form in which uncertainty occurs in the world. However, only since 1965 was a mathematical tool developed to formulate and deal with other forms of uncertainty. Fuzzy set theory was first introduced and published by Lotfi A. Zadeh [Zadeh,

1965]. Essentially, fuzzy set theory provides a natural approach to manipulating problems in which the transition between membership and nonmembership of the classes of objects is gradual rather than abrupt, and the source of imprecision is the absence of sharply defined class membership rather than the presence of random variables. In other words, it renders a methodology for dealing with phenomena that are vague, imprecise, too complex, or too ill defined to be susceptible to analysis by conventional mathematical and statistical means. The following material is mostly derived from Zadeh's papers [Zadeh, 1972, 1973, 1975] and includes the basic notions of the theory of fuzzy sets. For an extensive treatment of the general theory of fuzzy sets, refer to the Zadeh articles just cited, or other texts or monographs such as those by Kaufmann (1975), Negoita and Ralescu (1975), Dubois and Prade (1980), Zimmermann (1985, 1987), Yager et. al. (1987), and Novak (1989).

2.3.2 *Notation and Terminology*

In the following definitions, the signs /, +, Σ, and ∫ are used only as convenient notational forms and are not considered in their regular mathematical meanings.

Fuzzy Sets

Let R be the set of real numbers, and U be the universe of discourse, which is a collection of items of interest. Let u be a generic element of U. A fuzzy subset A of U is defined by a membership function μ_A: U → [0, 1] and [0, 1] denotes the closed unit interval on the real line. Then the fuzzy subset A of U can be expressed as follows:

$$A = \{\mu_{A(u)} / u;\ u \in U,\ \mu_{A(u)} \in [0,1]\}$$

In this case, the value $\mu_{A(u)}$ is referred to as the degree or grade of membership of u in A. Notice that a classical non-fuzzy set B can be considered a binary membership function $U \rightarrow \{0, 1\}$, where $\{0, 1\}$ is the set of values 0 and 1 rather than an interval.

Support

Let A be a fuzzy subset of U. The support of A, Supp (A), is the set of elements u in U whose membership in A $\mu_{A(u)}$ is positive. That is:

$$\mathrm{Supp}(A) = \{u / u \in U, \mu_{A(u)} > 0\}$$

Normality

A fuzzy subset A is normal if and only if $\mathrm{Supp}\mu_{A(u)} = 1$.

That is, the supremum over U is unity; otherwise, it is subnormal.

Fuzzy Singleton

A fuzzy singleton is a fuzzy set whose support is a single point in U. Suppose A is a fuzzy singleton whose support is the point u; then, we express A as

$$A = \mu / u$$

where μ is the grade of membership of u in A.

However, if A has finite support, say, $u_1, \ldots\ldots u_n$, and for each $i = 1, \ldots, n$, μ_i is the grade of membership of u_i in A, then A may be represented symbolically as a combination of fuzzy singletons by

$$A = \mu_1 / u_1 + \mu_2 / u_2 + \ldots\ldots + \mu_n / u_n$$

or more completely by

$$A = \sum_{i=1}^{n} \mu_i$$

A similar notation may be used in the case where the support is countable infinite. If the support is a continuum, then A may be denoted by

$$A = \int_U \frac{\mu_i}{u_i}$$

Fuzzy Cardinality

The fuzzy cardinality of a fuzzy set A on a finite universal set U is the summation of the membership grades of all the elements of U in A. Thus,

$$|A| = \sum_{u \in U} \mu_{A(u)}$$

α Level-Sets

If A is a fuzzy subset of U, then an α level-set of A is a non-fuzzy set denoted by A_α that comprises all elements of U whose grade of membership in A is greater than or equal to α.

In symbols:

$$A_\alpha = \{u / \mu_{A(u)} \geq \alpha, \alpha \in [0,1]\}$$

Fuzzy Number

A fuzzy number A is a fuzzy subset on the real line **R** such that its membership function μ_A is piecewise continuous and a_A, b_A, c_A, and d_A are elements of U:

i. $\mu_A(u) = 0$ for each $u \in (-\infty, c_A]$ U $[d_A, +\infty)$,

ii. μ_A is nondecreasing on $[c_A, a_A]$ and nonincreasing on $[b_A, d_A]$,

iii. $\mu_A(u) = 1$ for each $u \in [a_A, b_A]$.

Hamming Distance

Let S be an interval in R. The Hamming distance between two fuzzy subsets A and B on S is defined by the following:

$$D(A,B \mid S) = \int_{u \in S} \mid \mu_A(u) - \mu_B(u) \mid du$$

In case S = R, D(A, B|R) = D(A, B).

2.3.3 *Fuzzy Operations*

Let A and B be fuzzy subsets of a universe U, with membership functions μ_A and μ_B. Three of the major set operations have been generalized to fuzzy sets as follows.

Complement

The complement of A (denoted A') is defined by

$$A' = \sum_U (1 - \mu_A(u)) / u, u \in U$$

where Σ is used again as a convenient notational form.

Union

The union of A and B (denoted A ∪ B) is defined by:

$$A \cup B = \sum_U (\text{Max}[\mu_A(u), \mu_B(u)]) / u, u \in U$$

Intersection

The intersection of A and B (denoted A∩B) is defined by:

$$A \cap B = \sum_U (\text{Min}[\mu_A(u), \mu_B(u)]) / u, u \in U$$

The union corresponds to the connective "OR," whereas the intersection corresponds to the connective "AND," and the operation of complementation corresponds to negation.

Aggregation of Fuzzy Sets

Aggregation operations on fuzzy sets are operations by which several fuzzy sets are combined into a single set [Klir and Folger, 1988]. Thus, there exists a mapping such that

$$h:[0, 1]^{n} \rightarrow [0,1]$$

for some $n \geq 2$. When applied to n fuzzy sets defined on U, h produces an aggregate fuzzy set A by operating on the membership grades of each element of U in the aggregated sets.

In order to qualify as an aggregation function, the following two axiomatic requirements must be imposed on h [Dubois and Prade, 1985]:

- **Axiom 1:** Limit conditions:
  $h(0, 0, \ldots, 0) = 0$ and $h(1, 1, \ldots, 1) = 1$
- **Axiom 2:** Function h is monotonic nondecreasing; that is, for any pair a_i, b_i, where $a_i \in [0, 1]$ and $b_i \in [0, 1]$,
  if $a_i \geq b_i$ for all $i = 1, \ldots, q$, then $h(a_1, \ldots\ldots, a_q) \geq h(b_i, \ldots\ldots, b_q)$

Two additional axioms are usually employed to characterize aggregation operations [Klir and Folger, 1988]:

- **Axiom 3:** The equality of importance of all arguments aggregated must be satisfied [Yager, 1988]. This means that h should be symmetric with respect to its arguments.
- **Axiom 4:** h is a continuous function [Klir and Folger, 1988].

This axiom guarantees that an infinitesimal variation in any argument of h does not produce a noticeable change in the aggregate.

It can be shown [Dubois and Prade, 1985] that fuzzy unions and intersections qualify as aggregation operations on fuzzy sets. Although they are defined for only two arguments, their property of associativity guaranteed by their axioms provides a mechanism for extending their definition to any number of arguments. Thus, fuzzy unions and intersections can be viewed as special aggregation operations that are symmetric, usually continuous, and are required to satisfy some additional boundary conditions [Klir and Folger, 1988]. As a result of these additional requirements, the standard max (disjunctive attitude) and min (conjunctive attitude) operations represent boundaries between the averaging (compromise attitude) operations and the fuzzy unions and intersections, respectively [Dubois and Prade, 1985].

There are several classes of averaging operations [Yager, 1988]. They can be seen as a special family of generalized mean-like operations. They are symmetric, monotonic, and idempotent. One of them that covers the entire interval between the min and max operations consists of generalized means. That class of operations is defined as [Klir and Folger, 1988]

$$h_\alpha(a_1, a_2, \ldots a_n) = \left(\frac{a_1^\alpha + a_2^\alpha + \ldots + a_n^\alpha}{n} \right)^{\frac{1}{\alpha}}$$

where α is a parameter by which different means are distinguished, and $\alpha \in R$ $(\alpha \neq 0)$.

Function h_α clearly satisfies the two fundamental axioms (1 and 2) and the additional axioms (3 and 4). Consequently, it represents a parameterized class of continuous and symmetric aggregation operations.

Generalized Dombi operations [Dombi, 1982] form one of several classes of functions that possess appropriate axiomatic properties of fuzzy unions and intersections. The operations are defined in Chapter 4, "Computational Intelligence at Work," as they are very often utilized in applications.

2.3.4 *Cartesian Product*

A Cartesian product operation on two discrete fuzzy sets produces a membership function relational array. The array represents an implication about an output (conclusion) from a given input (antecedent). The Cartesian product is found by comparing pairs of membership values of the two fuzzy sets and selecting the minimum value of each pair.

Let A and B be two fuzzy sets, and R be the Cartesian product; then the operation is given by:

$$R = A \times B$$

The membership value of the Cartesian product is given by:

$$\mu_R = \text{Min}[\mu_A(a), \mu_B(b)]$$

Thus, each membership value in R is associated with an (a,b) pair.

Alternative relational relays may be formed in other ways. Here is an example:

$$\mu_R = \text{Max}\{\text{Min}[\mu_A(a), \mu_B(b)], (1 - \mu_A(a))\}$$

Under certain restricted conditions, these two expressions produce the same results. There are several other alternative formulations of relational arrays, but these two have been most often used in applications.

2.3.5 *Composition*

The array, R, obtained by the Cartesian product operation or one of its alternatives, relates (or maps) the elements of the fuzzy set A to the elements of fuzzy set B. Now, if the elements of the fuzzy set B are related to the elements of yet another fuzzy set, C, by another array, S, then it is possible to find an array that relates the elements of the fuzzy set A directly to the elements of the fuzzy set C. This array (say, T) is obtained by the composition

$$T = R \circ S$$

where the symbol ∘ denotes a fuzzy max-min composition. This may be expressed by a membership function:

$$\mu_T = \text{Max}[\text{Min}(\mu_R, \mu_S)]$$

2.3.6 *Extension Principle*

An extension principle enables mathematical functions of fuzzy sets to be defined and evaluated. The principle states that if a mathematical function is applied to a fuzzy set, then it should be applied to each of the fuzzy set elements.

Let there be a fuzzy set A, and let there be a function of the set f(A), where

$$A = [\mu_1 / a_1 + \mu_2 / a_2 + \mu_3 / a_3 + \mu_4 / a_4 + \ldots + \mu_n / a_n]$$

Then

$$f(A) = [\mu_1 / f(a_1) + \mu_2 / f(a_2) + \mu_3 / f(a_3) + \mu_4 / f(a_4) + \ldots + \mu_n / f(a_n)]$$

2.3.7 *Fuzzy Entropy Measures*

In general, a fuzzy entropy measure is the function f: P(X) → R, where P(X) denotes the set of all fuzzy subsets of X. That is, the function f assigns the value f(A) to each fuzzy subset A of X that characterizes the degree of fuzziness of A. Thus, f is a set-to-point map, or, in other words, a fuzzy set defined on fuzzy sets [Kosko, 1986].

Nonprobabilistic entropy was first defined by axioms in DeLuca and Termini (1972). Their axioms are intuitive and have been widely accepted in the fuzzy literature. We adopt them here.

In order to qualify as a meaningful measure of fuzziness, f must satisfy the following axiomatic requirements:

- **Axiom 1:** f(A) = 0 if and only if A is a crisp (non-fuzzy) set.
- **Axiom 2:** f(A) assumes the maximum if and only if A is maximally fuzzy.
- **Axiom 3:** If A is less fuzzy than B, then $f(A) \leq f(B)$.
- **Axiom 4:** $f(A) = f(A^c)$.

Only the first axiom is unique; axioms 2 and 3 depend on the meaning given to the concept of the degree of fuzziness. For example, assume that the *less fuzzy* relation is defined, after DeLuca and Termini (1972), as

$$\mu_A(x) \leq \mu_B(x) \text{ for } \mu_B(x) \leq 1/2$$
$$\mu_A(x) \geq \mu_B(x) \text{ for } \mu_B(x) \geq 1/2$$

and the term *maximally fuzzy* is defined by the membership grade 0.5 for all $x \in X$.

Motivated by the classical Shannon entropy function, DeLuca and Termini proposed the following fuzzy entropy function [DeLuca and Termini, 1972]:

$$f(A) = -\sum_{x \in X} (\mu_A(x) \log_2 \mu_A(x) + (1 - \mu_A(x)) \log_2 (1 - \mu_A(x)))$$

Its normalized version is given by f(A)/ [X], where [X] denotes the cardinality of the universal set X.

Similarly, taking into account the distance from set A to its complement A^C, another measure of fuzziness, referred to as an *index of fuzziness* [Kaufmann, 1975], can be introduced. If the "less fuzzy" relation of axiom 3 is defined by

$$\mu_c(x) = 0 \text{ if } \mu_A(x) \leq \tfrac{1}{2}$$

and

$$\mu_c(x) = 1 \text{ if } \mu_A(x) > \tfrac{1}{2}$$

where C is the crisp set nearest to the fuzzy set A, then the measure of fuzziness is expressed by the function [Kaufmann, 1975]

$$f(A) = \sum_{x \in X} [\mu_{A(x)} - \mu_{C(x)}]$$

when the Hamming distance is used, and by the function [Kaufmann, 1975]

$$f(A) = (\sum_{x \in X} [\mu_{A(x)} - \mu_{C(x)}]^2)^{1/2}$$

when the Euclidean distance is employed.

It is clear that other metric distances may be used as well [Klir and Folger, 1988]. For example, the Minkowski class of distances yields a class of fuzzy measures

$$f(A) = (\sum_{x \in X} [\mu_{A(x)} - \mu_{C(x)}]^w)^{1/w}$$

where $w \in [1, \infty]$.

However, both the DeLuca and Termini measure and the Kaufmann measure are only special cases of measures suggested in Knopfmacher (1975) and Loo (1977), expressed in the form [Klir and Folger, 1988]

$$f(A) = h(\sum_{x \in X} g_x(\mu_{A(x)}))$$

where g_x $(x \in X)$ are functions

$$g_x : [0,1] \rightarrow R^+$$

which are all monotonically increasing in [0, 0.5], monotonically decreasing in [0.5, 1], and satisfy the requirements that $g_x(0) = g_x(1) = 0$, and that $g_x(0.5)$ is the unique maximum of g_x, and h is a monotonically increasing function from R^+ to R^+.

It has been shown that the degree of fuzziness of a fuzzy set can be expressed in terms of the lack of distinction between the set and its complement [Yager, 1979, 1980; Higashi and Klir, 1982]. It has been also established that a general class of measures of fuzziness based on this lack of distinction is exactly the same as the class of measures of fuzziness expressed in terms of a metric distance based on some form of aggregating the individual differences [Klir and Folger, 1988]:

$$f_c(A) = [X] - \sum_{x \in X} [\mu_A(x) - c(\mu_A(x))]$$

To obtain the normalized version of fuzzy entropy, the preceding expression is divided by the cardinality of a fuzzy set.

The previous definitions can also be extended to infinite sets [Klir and Folger, 1988].

Another fuzzy entropy measure was proposed and investigated by Kosko [Kosko, 1986, 1992]. He established that

$$f(A) = \frac{\sum count(A \cap A^C)}{\sum count(A \cup A^C)}$$

where Σ count (sigma-count) is the fuzzy cardinality [Zadeh, 1983].

Kosko [Kosko, 1992] claims that his entropy measure, and corresponding fuzzy entropy theorem, does not hold when we substitute Zadeh's operations [Zadeh, 1965] with any other generalized fuzzy operations. If any of the generalized Dombi operations are used, the resulting measure is an entropy measure, it is maximized, but it does not equal unity at the midpoints [Cios and Sztandera, 1992].

The generalized Dombi operations proved to do well in different applications, and were used, among others in Cios and Sztandera (1993), for detecting coronary artery disease, and were suggested for image analysis in Sztandera (1990). However, we still have to use Zadeh's complement [Zadeh, 1965] because Kosko's theorem does not hold for any other class of fuzzy complements.

Application-based Concept of Fuzzy Entropy

In Chapter 4, the fuzzy entropy suggested in Kosko (1992) and generalized fuzzy operations introduced in Dombi (1982) are highlighted.

Generalized Dombi operations form one of several classes of functions that possess appropriate axiomatic properties of fuzzy unions and intersections.

As reported in [Cios and Sztandera, 1992], the parameter $\lambda = 4$ gives the best results.

It is interesting to examine the properties of these operations. By definition, generalized fuzzy union and intersection operations are commutative, associative, and monotonic. It can be shown that they satisfy neither the law of the excluded middle nor the law of contradiction. They are also not idempotent or distributive. However, they are continuous and satisfy de Morgan's laws (when the standard Zadeh complement is used) [Dombi, 1982]. Zadeh's complement ($c(a) = 1 - a$) is by definition monotonic nonincreasing. It is also continuous and involutive.

Other properties and the proofs can be found in the Dombi (1982) and Zadeh (1965) papers.

Fuzzy Trees

In the literature of fuzzy systems, several approaches to the idea of a fuzzy tree have been introduced. A very good overview of the literature and a general approach to fuzzy tree problems can be found in Delgado et. al. (1990). The authors establish two problem groups into which all fuzzy tree publications fall. Group one defines properties of the classical concept of the fuzzy tree framework, and group two considers the fuzzy tree as a representation of an imprecise relation between items and uses the properties of connectedness. A concept in Rosenfeld (1975) is representative of the first group, and an approach in McAllister (1987) represents the second.

From these two types, three different fuzzy tree models can be introduced:

- **Fuzzy edge tree**—This tree is based on the following concept: If we are given a complete tree G, a fuzzy tree F of G is a tree in which a fuzzy membership degree is attached to each edge of the tree. The degree μ_e expresses the degree of edge e belonging to tree F. So, if $\mu_e = 0$, the edge does not belong to F; if $\mu_e = 1$, the edge belongs fully to F, and all other cases represent intermediate fuzzy edges. This model is referenced as belonging to group two.
- **Fuzzy vertex tree**—A fuzzy vertex tree is based on yet another concept. If we are given an arbitrary (crisp) reference tree G, a fuzzy tree F to every vertex in G is a tree in which a fuzzy membership degree is assigned to each vertex of the tree. The degree μ_e, in this case, represents the degree obtained by any aggregation operation performed on membership degrees of the vertices connected by an edge. This approach was introduced in Koczy (1992).
- **Fuzzy vertex and edge tree**—This model allows the attachment of fuzzy membership degrees both to vertices and edges. It was originally introduced in Rosenfeld (1975), but is quite

complicated to have any practical value for solving problems. In this model the resultant degree, representing the membership of an edge e, is always a function of its own degree and the two degrees attached to the vertices connected by the common edge. The resultant grade of membership is obtained by performing an aggregation operation on the three aforementioned degrees. For our purposes, none of the three aforementioned concepts are applicable. They cannot be used to convert decision trees into hidden layers of a neural network [Cios and Sztandera, 1993]. Because the FCID3 algorithm needs to generate fuzzy subsets, instead of one grade of membership, a new concept of a fuzzy tree is introduced next.

Application-based Concept of a Fuzzy Tree

An application-based concept of a fuzzy tree was developed and implemented in order to execute ranking of fuzzy subsets at nodes of hidden layers of a neural network [Sztandera, 1993]. Such a decision tree has fuzzy subsets at each of its nodes (vertices). Each fuzzy subset consists of several grades of membership. Even though it may seem to be computationally more difficult to deal with the fuzzy subsets, the incorporation of a fuzzy tree in the CID3 [Cios and Liu, 1992] algorithm has given better results, both in reducing the neural network structure and in convergence [Cios and Sztandera, 1993]. This fuzzy tree has fuzzy subsets at every node but the root node. The subsets descending from a parent node are in the same graph because they are used in the ranking processes.

2.4 Genetic Algorithms

Genetic algorithms (GAs) are optimization searches first introduced by Holland (1975). As the name suggests, they were inspired by the observation of processes occurring in natural evolution. They mimic the processes, and as such are utilized in solving optimization problems. In general, genetic algorithms perform directed random searches through a given set of alternatives with the aim of finding the best alternative with respect to given criteria. These criteria are expressed in terms of an objective function, referred to as a "fitness function."

Genetic algorithms are a computational intelligence technique based on the biological concepts of natural selection and genetics [Holland, 1975]. In this approach, the variables that define the solution to a complex problem are represented as genes on a chromosome. GAs feature a group of candidate solutions (a "population" of solutions) on the response surface. Through a form of natural selection and the genetic operations of mutation and recombination, chromosomes with better fitness are generated. Natural selection creates pressure that encourages the better chromosomes to propagate into future populations. Using the recombination operator, a GA combines genes from two parent chromosomes to form two new chromosomes with a high probability that a solution of superior fitness will result. Mutation allows new areas of the response surface to be explored. GAs offer a generational improvement in the fitness of the chromosomes and, after many generations, will create chromosomes containing optimum or near-optimum variable settings.

A genetic algorithm encompasses four important steps:

1. The initial population of chromosomes is created either randomly or by perturbing an input chromosome.
2. In the evaluation step, the fitness is computed using either a function derived from a summation of the properties of individual genes or the more sophisticated Bohachevsky function [Bohachevsky et. al., 1986].
3. The next step is the exploitation or natural selection step. Chromosomes with the largest fitness scores are placed

ochastically into a mating subset. Chromosomes with iess scores are removed from the population. A binary nent mating subset selection method could be used.

4. The final step, exploration, involves use of recombination and mutation operators. Two chromosomes from the mating subset are randomly selected and, using the uniform crossover method, recombination is applied. Steps 2 through 4 are repeated for a predetermined number of generations, or until a solution of suitable quality has been located.

Genetic algorithms search for the best alternative through the evolution of chromosomes, and produce the best offspring with respect to the given criteria. Thus, tackling big data makes it feasible for genetic algorithms to produce unconventional outcomes managers might not consider. This is of paramount importance to innovative businesses. Genetic algorithms can serve as a powerful tool that allows the best alternatives to emerge (sometimes before reasons for them become apparent), evolve, and subsequently be leveraged to gain a competitive edge.

2.5 Neuro-Fuzzy Systems

2.5.1 Introduction

Years after the idea of fuzziness was introduced by Zadeh (1965), many scientists and engineers felt that this was yet another new and bizarre technology with little to offer other than vacuous theories, uninteresting projects, and lots of graduate students! Although non-vacuous fuzzy theories have indeed grown in almost all conceivable directions since 1965, the proof of any new technology ultimately lies in its utility for solving real problems. Models based on Zadeh's idea have emerged as an enabling technology for many commercially successful products using fuzzy control and fuzzy pattern recognition.

Sophisticated applications to complex problems in many domains are well on the way to becoming parts of fielded systems.

Neural networks, neuro-computing, or "brain-like" computation is based on the wishful hope that we can reproduce at least some of the flexibility and power of the human brain by artificial means. Neural networks consist of many simple computing elements—generally simple nonlinear summing junctions—joined together by connections of varying strength (weights), a gross abstraction of the brain, which consists of very large numbers of far more complex neurons connected together with far more complex and far more structured couplings.

One of the computational intelligence avenues joins together the two aforementioned techniques—neural networks and fuzzy systems. They are parallel in nature and share the common ability to work well in this natural environment. From an engineering point of view, much of the interest in neural networks and fuzzy systems has been for dealing with difficulties arising from uncertainty, imprecision, and noise. The more a problem resembles those encountered in the real world—and most interesting problems do—the better the system must cope with these difficulties.

The marriage of fuzzy logic with artificial neural networks (ANNs) has a sound technical basis, because these two approaches generally attack the design of "intelligent" systems from quite different angles. ANNs are essentially low-level, computational algorithms that offer good performance in dealing with sensor data used in pattern recognition and control. On the other hand, fuzzy logic was introduced as a means for representing, manipulating, and utilizing data and information that possess nonstatistical uncertainty. Thus, fuzzy methods often deal with issues such as reasoning on a higher (semantic or linguistic) level than ANNs. Consequently, the two technologies often complement each other: ANNs supply the brute force necessary to accommodate and interpret large amounts of sensor data, and fuzzy logic provides a structural framework that utilizes and exploits these low-level results.

What is most important, however, is that there seem to be many ways to use either technology as a "tool" within the framework of a model based on the other. For example, an artificial neural network is well known for its ability to represent functions. The basis of every fuzzy model is the membership function. Therefore, a natural application of ANNs in fuzzy models is to provide good approximations to the membership functions that are essential to the success of any fuzzy approach.

2.5.2 A Need for Fuzzy Set Theory Approaches in Neural Network Structures

Neural network architectures cover a wide range. In one sense, every computer is a neural net, because we can view traditional digital logic as constructed from McCulloch-Pitts "neurons" [McCulloch and Pitts, 1943]. They were proposed in 1943 as models of biological neurons and arranged in networks for the specific purpose of computing logic functions. The architectures of current neural networks are massively parallel and concerned with approximating input-output relationships, with many units arranged in large parallel arrays computing simultaneously. Massive parallelism is of great importance now that the speed of light begins to constrain computers of standard serial design. Large-scale parallelism provides a way to significantly increase computer speed. Even limited understanding and crude approximations into how the brain combines slow and noisy computing devices into powerful systems can offer considerable insight.

Self-generating neural networks can perform interesting and useful computations if we choose the problem appropriately. Indeed, the problems where artificial neural networks have the most promise are those with a real-world flavor: prediction, pattern recognition, and classification.

Artificial neural networks help to solve these problems with natural mechanisms of generalization. To oversimplify, suppose we represent an object in a network as a pattern of activation of several units. If a unit or two in a large network responds incorrectly, the overall pattern stays pretty much the same, and the network still responds correctly to stimuli. Or, if an object, once seen, reappears, but slightly different, then the pattern of activation representing the object closely resembles its previous appearance, and the network still tends to respond almost as it did before. When neural networks operate, similar inputs naturally produce similar outputs. Most real-world perceptual problems have this structure of input-output continuity.

If neural networks show intrinsic generalization, we might wonder if we could observe similar effects in human psychology. The "prototype" model provides a scheme for human categorization with a good deal of psychological support. Instead of forming a property list for a category, we store a "best example" of the category (or possibly a few best examples). The system computes the similarity between a new example and the prototype, and classifies the new example as an example of the category in the nearest neighbor sense—if the new example is "close enough" to the prototype. Computational neural networks naturally develop this kind of category structure. In fact, we can hardly stop neural networks from doing it, which points out a serious potential weakness of some particular kinds of neural networks. Classification by similarity causes neural networks great distress in situations where we cannot trust similarity.

A difficult example is a "parity" problem—where there is an even or odd number of ones in a binary vector. Parity changes if one element in a vector is changed. Parity causes no difficulties for digital logic. However, it was impossible for simple neural networks to compute the parity function in the 1960s, which caused the engineering community to lose interest in neural networks.

Algorithmic techniques for dealing with uncertainty are sometimes as much statements about human psychology as they are about algorithms. Artificial neural networks deal with uncertainty as humans do, not by deliberate design, but as a byproduct of their parallel distributed structure. It would be equally possible, and perhaps desirable, for us to directly build these insights about categorization into an artificial system. Fuzzy systems take this approach.

Fuzzy or multivalued set theory develops the basic insight that categories are not absolutely clear cut: A particular example of a category can "belong" to a lesser or greater degree to that category. This assumption captures quite nicely the psychological observation that a particular object can be a better or worse example of a model, depending on other members of the category.

Traditional probability theory assumes an accuracy and precision of categorization of the world that may not represent many important problems. We must wonder what would have happened if, instead of being concerned with gambling or insurance, for example, probability theory had been initially developed to predict the weather, where there are continuous gradations between overlapping linguistic categories: dense fog, drizzle, light rain, heavy rain, and downpour. Perhaps fuzzy systems would have become the mainstream of uncertainty reasoning formalisms and "traditional" probability an extreme approximation useful in certain special cases. The reaction of most people when they first hear about fuzzy logic is the feeling that this formulation makes sense psychologically.

Artificial neural networks process numerical information and exhibit learning capabilities. Fuzzy systems can process linguistic information and represent experts' knowledge in the form of fuzzy rules or fuzzy reasoning architectures such as fuzzy trees. Therefore, it is not surprising that the fusion of these two technologies is a very interesting research topic. The aim is to create algorithms and then their hardware implementations that will behave "intelligently." In this research effort, we are interested in merging the aforementioned technologies.

Neural networks can be used to produce membership functions for fuzzy sets from numerical data. Moreover, one can take advantage of the learning capability of neural networks to manipulate those membership functions (say, for classification and pattern recognition processes, prediction, or for ranking in multicriteria decision making, which occurs frequently in the real world). In the opposite direction, one can use fuzzy reasoning architecture, such as fuzzy trees, to construct neural networks.

The fusion of neural networks and fuzzy systems is essentially based on the fact that neural networks can learn experts' knowledge through numerical data, and fuzzy systems can represent experts' knowledge through the representation of in-out relations by fuzzy reasoning.

As in any science, practical successes call for theoretical justifications. Although the previous technologies have become firmly established in well-defined domains of applications, only a few theoretical results have been obtained. Theoretical results are needed, not only for explaining successful results but also for guiding general design methodology for systems. The success of neural networks is explained by the universal approximation property of the Stone-Weierstrass theorem [Hornik et. al., 1989; Cybenko, 1989; Hornik, 1991]. However, there is no standard method for determining the number of neural units in hidden layers.

Mathematically speaking, although the graphical form of neural networks indicates that such input-output maps can approximate continuous functions to any degree of accuracy, one still faces the practical problem of what specific network structure will actually do the job.

A common approach to supervised classification and prediction in artificial intelligence and statistical pattern recognition is the use of decision trees. A tree is "grown" from data using a recursive partitioning algorithm to create a tree that, hopefully, has good prediction of classes on new data. Standard algorithms in the realm of ANNs are "tiling" by Nadal [Nadal, 1989], the algorithm of Bischel and Seitz [Bischel and Seitz, 1989], and the CID3 [Cios and Liu, 1992].

A valuable computational intelligence approach—ANN algorithm that can be used for the creation and manipulation of fuzzy membership functions—could be utilized to gain a competitive advantage in decision making. In the opposite direction, a decision fuzzy tree could be converted to a corresponding artificial neural network.

Conclusions

In this chapter, a brief overview of the basic concepts of artificial neural networks, fuzzy sets, and genetic algorithms, as well as neuro-fuzzy systems, to be used in subsequent chapters, was given. Interested readers are referred to Zadeh (1965), Kaufmann, (1975), Negoita and Ralescu (1975), Dubois and Prade (1980), Zimmermann (1985, 1987), Yager et. al. (1987), Novak (1989), Rumelhart et. al. (1986), and Holland (1975) for more detailed presentations.

Exercises

1. Artificial Neural Networks

   1.1. [Level 1] Explore a basic perceptron model for artificial neural networks. Discuss its limitations, and suggest ways to overcome them.

   1.2. [Level 2] It can be shown that the perceptron learning rule for the single-neuron perceptron will always converge to weights that accomplish the desired classification (assuming that such weights exist). Provide a proof of convergence.

2. Artificial Neural Networks

   2.1. [Level 1] Conduct a literature review on supervised and unsupervised learning algorithms. Highlight advantages and disadvantages of each approach.

   2.2. [Level 2] Propose and design an artificial neural network that could address one of your business problems. Explain how your system differentiates from existing programs.

   2.3. [Level 3] Implement your program.

   2.4. [Level 4] Field-test your program with a business partner. If the test proves successful, consider steps to commercialize it.

3. Artificial Neural Networks

   [Level 1] Conduct a literature review on applications of artificial neural networks that could be potentially utilized in your company.

4. Fuzzy Sets

   [Level 1] Explain the difference between randomness and fuzziness, and provide an example for each.

5. Fuzzy Sets

   5.1. [Level 1] Provide examples of extension principle utilization.

5.2. [Level 2] Propose and design a fuzzy system that addresses one of your business problems. Explain how your system differentiates from existing programs and highlight the advantages of the fuzzy system.

6. Fuzzy Sets

[Level 1] Conduct a literature review on applications of fuzzy sets in your industry.

7. Fuzzy Sets

Engineering thermodynamics derives from classical thermodynamics. It is defined as a system with a continuous surface boundary defined by an observer, and is in thermodynamic equilibrium with its surroundings. Thermodynamic equilibrium means thermal, chemical, mechanical, as well as, in general, gravitational, magnetic, and electrical equilibrium.

A thermodynamic state of the system is defined by its properties, such as temperature, pressure, specific volume, entropy, and enthalpy. In turn, the properties of a substance are defined by empirical equations of state, which are valid over limited ranges and verified by experimentally determined values. Thermodynamic properties can only be defined in a state of equilibrium, although they are sometimes used in processes that are far from equilibrium. Instrument readings of properties may then only be approximately in accord with the theoretical predictions. Ideal processes are defined in classical thermodynamics. Although those processes are theoretically reversible, they are unattainable in reality and serve as limits to actual processes, which are always irreversible.

From the preceding it is clear that uncertainty is present in calculations related to real thermodynamic processes, and why even under the best possible physical conditions, the observations may only correspond approximately to theoretical calculations. In general, thermodynamic properties could be then more properly represented by fuzzy sets [Harris, 2000]. Fuzzy sets are used to deal with uncertainty in engineering and science problems, where uncertainty is not of random nature, and the corresponding concepts are of possibility rather than probability theory.

7.1. [Level 1] Conduct a literature review on applications of fuzzy sets in the solar energy industry.

7.2. [Level 2] Explore the foundations of a solar energy system and express the variables and processes in terms of fuzzy sets. Define the principles behind the solar water heater, and subsequently design a fuzzy set model for it.

8. Fuzzy Sets

[Level 3] The explosive growth of the Internet has made huge amounts of information available to decision makers. The lack of a query language descriptive enough to allow a user to precisely express his or her desires, compounded by the highly diverse structure of the documents on the Web, makes the task of finding a specific piece of information often laborious and time consuming. However, one task that search engines are good at is retrieving a large number of documents related to a particular subject of interest. This leads one to consider the possibility of having software that can integrate and summarize the information retrieved, and present it in a coherent and cohesive way to the user. The full realization of this is, at the very least, bounded by our current ability in text understanding. Although we can easily locate key words in text documents, we might not extract the critical parts of documents to integrate and summarize multiple pieces of information.

The challenge here is to develop software that can provide a limited type of summarization of the information contained in multiple retrieved documents. Central to this approach is the use of fuzzy set technology to act as a bridge, helping to convert the difficult task of text summarization into the easier problem of numeric summarization.

Use the latest technologies from data and text mining, fuzzy sets, ontologies, and the semantic web to enable the building of an information-gathering system that's more sophisticated than the existing search engines—a system that will play an important role in the strategic planning of companies across different industries. Using recent results from the aforementioned technologies, the system should examine online, open Internet sources that contain information about emerging patterns and trends, brand monitoring, new product feedback, assessing impact of advertising, image management, and emergent ideas. It should overcome existing barriers in Google, Yahoo!, and other search engines by using ontologies to provide a deeper, more human-like understanding of the information.

Using methods from fuzzy sets, the system should summarize this information in a manner that is easily understood by a managerial-type decision maker. The possessor of this kind of information will have an important advantage in being able to respond rapidly and appropriately in making critical decisions. During your research, which could lead to your graduate thesis or dissertation, you should provide a general architecture for a "buzz" mining system, and should develop the underlying technology needed to build and test a prototype system.

9. Neuro-Fuzzy Systems

Fuzzy systems and artificial neural networks, both model-free systems, contain their own advantages and drawbacks. One area of combining them, known as neuro-fuzzy systems, seeks maximization of the desirable properties and the reduction of disadvantages in both systems.

9.1. [Level 1] Conduct a literature review of commercial applications of neuro-fuzzy systems.

9.2. [Level 2] Compare different learning strategies utilized in neuro-fuzzy systems, and provide recommendations for possible applications.

9.3. [Level 3] Work out all the details and outline an artificial neural network algorithm that can be used for the creation and manipulation of fuzzy membership functions. Explain how it could subsequently be utilized to gain a competitive edge in decision making. Prove that in the opposite direction, a decision fuzzy tree could be converted to a corresponding artificial neural network.

10. Genetic Algorithms

[Level 1] Conduct a literature review on the applications of genetic algorithms in business.

11. Genetic Algorithms

[Level 4] In communities across the nation, there is a growing concern that current development patterns, dominated by what some call "sprawl," are no longer in the long-term interest of our cities, existing suburbs, small towns, rural communities, and wilderness areas. Sprawl is land development patterns characterized by fragmented and segregated land uses, low-density residential settlements, widespread strip commercial development along roadways, and the lack of connectivity within and between neighborhoods. Though often supportive of growth, communities are questioning the economic and environmental costs of abandoning infrastructure in the city, only to rebuild it further out.

As noted by the U.S. Environmental Protection Agency and several other agencies and organizations, "smart growth" incorporates a number of principles that contrast with sprawl: mixing land uses; taking advantage of compact building design; creating a range of housing opportunities and choices; creating walkable neighborhoods; fostering distinctive, attractive communities with a strong sense of place; preserving open space, farmland, natural beauty, and critical environmental areas; strengthening and directing development toward existing communities; providing a variety of transportation choices; making development decisions predictable, fair, and cost effective; and encouraging community and stakeholder collaboration in development decisions. Smart growth invests time, attention, and resources in restoring community and vitality to existing cities and older suburbs. Smart growth in new developments is more town centered, is auto accessible but also accommodates transit and pedestrian activity, and has a greater mix of housing, commercial, and retail uses. It also preserves open space and protects sensitive areas such as wetlands. Smart growth recognizes connections between development and quality of life.

Propose a research project for your Ph.D. dissertation that will support the construction and deployment of a sophisticated, multiobjective genetic algorithm-based model to holistically understand and predict the effects of suburban growth on communities across the country. Incorporate several existing models (e.g., storm water management, traffic congestion, and biodiversity) to study and communicate the interdependency of the full range of environmental and economic factors. Evaluate different community growth scenarios over long periods of time and, thereby, allow stakeholders (e.g., planners, civic leaders, and citizens) to balance and prioritize trade-offs between the desire for a more sustainable society (public sector) and economically viable communities (private sector).

3

Computational Intelligence Versus Statistical Approaches

Learning Objectives

- To understand the difference between computational intelligence and statistical models
- To gain insights into computational intelligence by learning the conditions under which it could be used
- To understand when computational intelligence has an upper hand over statistical approaches
- To understand that computational intelligence is needed when managers face big data problems and are uncertain of the assumptions needed to specify consequences and impact of decision alternatives
- To appreciate the power of computational intelligence in adding value to one's business

3.1 Introduction

Although most (if not all) literature on big data analysis utilizes statistical software packages, this book urges managers to take advantage of computational intelligence for analysis, exploration, and knowledge generation. The computational intelligence approach is needed as companies gather enormous amounts of data that are increasingly both heterogeneous and unstructured, often coming from complex networks extending to both suppliers and customers. This creates potentially rather complex relationships between all the entities.

Computational intelligence is different from statistical approaches in many ways. Analysis involving all five types of data—numbers, text, images, audio, and video—requires integration, clustering, and decision making derived from computational intelligence rather than generating predefined reports based on statistical inferences.

Computational intelligence tools have a multitude of real world applications. They are well suited to dissect and analyze big data and extract meaningful, at times hidden, patterns and relationships. The advantages of computational intelligence tools over statistical models are

- They require no predefined knowledge of underlying relationships between input and output variables.
- Their associative ability makes them robust enough to tolerate missing and inaccurate data.
- Their performance does not diminish with multi-colinearity problems, violations of set assumptions, high influence points, and transformation problems encountered in regression analysis.

Large enterprises strive to stay competitive by strategically utilizing modern day data analytics to understand and to be closely in tune with the changing needs and preferences of their customers. Statistics (moving averages, ratio analysis, time series analysis, and regression analysis) and applied mathematics techniques (linear programming, calculus, and simulation tools) greatly enhance the businesses' ability to dissect the given data and organize it to create meaningful information to support decision making. However, all these methods require human intervention to

- organize appropriate data;
- analyze meaningful information;
- and communicate useful knowledge.

This process is time consuming and, worse yet, *static*—meaning that the result of analysis is specific to the time frame of analysis. The computational intelligence approach provides an attractive alternative that enables large businesses to be adaptive to the changing needs and preferences for each customer segment.

3.2 Adding Value to Business Through Utilization of Computational Intelligence

Many innovative businesses have taken advantage of computational intelligence approaches to identify specific customers and subsequently pursuing them rather than waiting for them to respond to passive appeals. Computational intelligence allows for identifying customers that are most likely to respond to the appeals. It provides decision makers with likelihood coefficients, thus quantifying customers' response rate. Some of the common areas of applying computational intelligence include the following:

- Customer segmentation for direct marketing
- Customer profiling for relationship management
- Efficient mailing campaigns
- Customer retention
- Identification of cross-selling opportunities
- Credit score analysis
- Detection of fraudulent behavior and transactions

All of these applications rely on massive internal as well as external data sets. Because many of the potentially differentiating features are not collected by businesses for internal purposes, it is essential to tap into vast external resources. Those pieces of data, coupled with internal data, provide a way to form information. Subsequently, those pieces of information, clustered around a specific subject or object, form knowledge that could be utilized for decision making.

The additional information could be drawn from multiple providers that collect and analyze demographic, socio-graphic, as well as business data. Many business management systems rely on real-time access to credit bureau data sets as well as secondary demographic and sociographic data repositories. Some of them employ computational intelligence modules, including artificial neural networks such as Minotaur [Neural Technologies, 2014] or fuzzy sets such as Ghost Miner [Fujitsu, 2014]. These capabilities empower organizations to improve bottom-line profits in many business avenues. They provide tools for the following tasks:

- Optimizing market research and marketing efforts
- Extracting maximum profit from existing customers through cross- and up-selling
- Managing customer attrition rates
- Assessing customers for bad debt/fraud at the application stage (originations)
- Detecting concealed fraudulent activities
- Identifying and reducing fraud from customers, outsiders, and employees
- Streamlining collections procedures
- Locating debtors quickly and efficiently
- Managing credit risk throughout the customer's lifetime
- Ensuring all revenue generated is correctly billed and accounted for

Utilization of computational intelligence techniques in business management systems has provided dramatic increases in return on investment and in profits for companies, savings that could go into the millions of dollars.

Computational intelligence approaches for big data analysis have also been employed by law enforcement for quite some time now. In the Camden/Philadelphia HIDTA (High Intensity Drug Trafficking Agency), computational intelligence approaches were utilized to enhance existing networks toward cross-referencing criminal records, case files, and other relevant crime information into a region encompassing three states, over a dozen counties, and a multitude of local jurisdictions [Lutz, 2002].

Money laundering enforcement operations in many countries have developed, from the simple use of informant information to the sophisticated analysis of voluminous, complex financial transaction arrays [Watkins, 2003]. The volume of those records and the complexity of the relationships called for innovative techniques that could aid financial investigators in generating timely, accurate leads. Computational intelligence techniques are well suited for identifying trends and patterns in large data sets that are often composed of tens of thousands of complex hidden relationships.

It seems that eyes are the reflection of the mind. Researchers and data scientists have always been interested in eyes' reactions, being interpreted as outside gates for the mind. An enormous variety of techniques have already been tested and used for different purposes. The use of eye tracking to study human perceptual processes and preferences crosses many disciplines, from neuroscience and psychology to marketing and advertising, from computer science to human factors research. Nowadays, eye tracking has become more available to marketing research firms, as devices have become more available, cheaper, and simpler.

Eye tracking can be used by marketing research firms to show clients what parts of the screen or an advertisement will attract customer attention. So-called *bee swarms*, when multiple records of individuals' eye movements are brought together into a visual swarm, are often used to analyze what consumers typically focus on when looking at advertisements or commercials. The results provide clues about the effectiveness of particular images and their relationships to a product, brand name, and other features, even in video streams. Multiple eye tracking streams can be represented in various visual displays, including heat maps, which show which areas of a visual draw the most attention; cloud maps, which show what viewers do and do not look at; gaze plots, which show the usual path of a viewer's eyes from point to point in a visual; and zone analysis, which breaks a visual or page into colored zones based on the strongest areas of interest.

In terms of new product development, the future potential of eye tracking for interactive design is enormous—especially when one considers its potential for commercial use. The ability to customize design, without the need to formally describe it, would open many doors for distributed design, which goes well in pair with the increases in distributed fabrication through 3D printers. This could potentially allow hands-free design by passively gathering user feedback via eye tracking, as long as the technology accurately infers which object the user is looking at, and using that information to direct successful design sessions. Users could successfully design target objects and could produce interesting, novel shapes without touching a keyboard or mouse. National Science Foundation (NSF) and other government agencies are known to have sponsored research in that area.

The next chapter will highlight examples of applications of computational intelligence. These examples contain transferrable lessons to many other industries and problems. They could be made to work for your problems, thus creating further value for your businesses.

Exercises

1. Observation research represents one of many qualitative market research approaches. One of the techniques used in observation research is eye tracking. Eye tracking yields valuable information about which features are most "eye catching." Online advertising can use this to pinpoint the best ad placement on a web page.

   1.1. [Level 1] Outline the possible utilization of computational intelligence in eye-tracking research.

   1.2. [Level 2] Design a computational intelligence–based eye tracking system that could be used to improve ad placement in online advertising. Explain how your system differentiates from existing algorithms.

   1.3. [Level 3] Implement your program.

   1.4. [Level 4] Field-test your program with a business partner. If the test proves successful, consider steps to commercialize it.

2. Fraud can be defined as a criminal activity, involving false representations to gain an unjust return. Fraud occurs in a wide variety of ways, and is ever changing as new technologies and ubiquitous use of social media create new opportunities for fraudulent activity. Computational intelligence algorithms are often part of the most comprehensive fraud detection systems used by businesses nowadays.

   2.1. [Level 1] Conduct a literature review on fraud detection systems. Compare and contrast the ways statistical and computational intelligence techniques address and solve the problem.

   2.2. [Level 2] Design a computational intelligence–based fraud detection system focusing on one or several aspects of fraudulent activities. Explain how your system differentiates from existing programs.

2.3. [Level 3] Implement your program.

2.4. [Level 4] Field-test your program with a business partner. If the test proves successful, consider starting a company to implement and market it. Perform needs analysis to identify whether there is demand for the outputs of the activity in a specific market or community. The aim of the analysis is to prove there is demand for the particular activity you are proposing to deliver. This will help to reduce the possibility of a failure of the activity, or the activity not producing the results anticipated on a larger scale, thus leading to a loss on investment.

3. [Level 2] Itemize the business development tools you use in your projects. Consider augmenting your tools with computational intelligence. For each such identified opportunity, answer the following questions:

   3.1. What functionality would it provide that is not yet available in the market?

   3.2. What functionality of other available tools does it duplicate?

   3.3. How does the capability of this tool, and the availability of commercial sources for this capability (or lack of it), impact the prospect of transferring your insights to business practice?

4. [Level 4] Implement your next project in a business development environment that meets as many of your business requirements and constraints as possible. Explore ways to package the additional functionality you require as add-ons to this environment. Transfer these add-ons to the vendor of the development environment for them to make available in the next released version of their product.

4

Computational Intelligence at Work

Learning Objectives

- To demonstrate an understanding of theory and selected research topics in the computational intelligence field
- To gain an ability to apply, through the cited examples, transferrable lessons to many other industries and problems
- To utilize the examples of computational intelligence at work, and to improve upon them, so they create further value for your business

4.1 Introduction

Businesses and managers face significant challenges in processing big data sets that are being further augmented on a daily basis. Computational intelligence tools allow for processing those data, verifying many of the managers' intuitions, discovering and evaluating new patterns, and basing decisions on data. The tools provide an unprecedented opportunity for knowledge discovery and theory development. Never before have organizations had data of the variety and scale available today. Some of the applications are highlighted in this chapter.

4.2 Role of Analytics in Medical Informatics

Computational intelligence has a valuable predictive power and enables clinicians to determine, with an acceptable level of accuracy, the proper diagnosis, treatment protocol, or medicine dosage. Classification is the most often used technique utilizing analytics in medical informatics. Analytics can have a profound effect in medical informatics. Computational intelligence is not a "magic bullet," though, for a given study. Therefore, it is recommended that a thorough evaluation of applications be undertaken before committing to an approach. Some of the potential applications are highlighted in this section.

4.2.1 Classification Data Mining with Hybrid Fuzzy Logic Aggregation

The first application involves fuzzy logic being applied to the category discrimination problem related to the identification of mammary lesions as benign or malignant [Sanford and Sztandera, 2011]. Results of other similar studies are reviewed for comparison purposes. The current analysis expands the fuzzy logic approach by using the normal distribution function as set membership functions and using a genetic algorithm to optimize performance with the training partition.

The approach is applicable to problems having an arbitrarily large number of parameters. Two different data sets are examined. Data are portioned into a training set and validation set, and each set is segregated into benign and malignant records. Values of mean and standard deviation are initially computed from the associated attributes and are different for the benign and malignant records. In one training method, the standard deviations are adjusted to minimize overall error. In the second method, bias adjusts the importance of each membership function.

Defuzzification is accomplished in three ways: a modified averaging and OR process, comparison of the multiplied fuzzy set values, and comparison of the multiplied squared set values. The results are compared with results obtained through statistical logistic regression.

Since its introduction in 1965 by Zadeh [Zadeh, 1965], the fuzzy set theory has found extensive application in control systems, from small appliances to cameras and even heavy equipment. Although control systems are its forte, not surprisingly it has found its way into most if not all areas of data mining as a seriously competing analytic tool. To this repertoire, I would add numerous information search and utilization techniques, which have even spawned a fuzzy database query language developed by Takihashi [Takihashi, 1995].

Fuzzy logic shows itself to great advantage when it can simplify an otherwise extremely difficult algebraic formulation for a control system without apparent loss of effectiveness. In fact, the fuzzy approach may be more effective. For example, in the automatic control of a camera, the input parameters are light intensity, distance to object, motion of the object relative to the camera, and the capability of the recording media. Of these, the only constant parameter is the capability of the recording media. Other parameters may exhibit variations over a wide range. Formulation of a crisp (exact) control system is quite difficult. The fuzzy approach classifies the input parameters into fuzzy sets. For example, these sets might be "dim light," "medium light," "bright light," "nearby," "some distance," and "remote distance." The task then is to determine the percent of membership that the actual parameter has in each associated set. For example, light may have 80% membership in "medium," 10 % membership in "bright," and zero membership in "dim." The setting of camera speed and aperture then is based on linguistic rules. One such rule might be, "If there is a bright light and it is at a remote distance and there is zero relative motion, then the aperture setting is 16 and the corresponding speed is 1/100." Another might be, "If there is a medium light and it is at a remote distance and there is zero relative motion, then the aperture setting is 11 and the corresponding speed is 1/100."

Linguistic rules are logic statements. They include intersection and union. Typically these are resolved through a set of rules, as follows:

- A AND B, where A and B are limited to the range (0, 1), becomes equivalent to min (A, B).
- A OR B, where A and B are limited to the range (0, 1), becomes equivalent to max (A, B).

The capability of classifying patterns for subsequent decision-making processes is one of the most fundamental characteristics of business intelligence and data mining. As a field of study, classification has been evolving since the early 1950s, closely following the emergence and evolution of computer technology and classification techniques. As previously mentioned, fuzzy logic has been applied to this type of problem.

Fuzzy Data Discrimination

The topic of fuzzy data discrimination has led to a profusion of articles. We mention a few that deal with medical diagnosis, which is also the direction of the current work.

Cios (1994) reported on fuzzy sets used for classification of coronary stenosis from planar thallium-201 scintigraphs. The research was focused on diagnosis of stenosis, which might be occurring in any of the three major arteries: the left anterior descending (LAD), the right coronary artery (RCA), or the circumflex artery (CCX). The scintigraphy consisted of three views: left ventricle-anterior (ANT), left lateral

(LAT), and anterior oblique (LAO). These data are themselves fuzzy with considerable overlap in perfusion patterns that might be created by stenosis. Some other approaches to solving this problem include fuzzy sets with probability assigned membership functions, machine learning algorithms, and an expert system approach [Cios et. al., 1990, 1991, 1994]. We focus here on diagnosis of coronary artery stenosis based on T1-201 scintigraphs.

T1-201 Scintigraphs Data

Stress T1-201 scintigraphs were obtained from patients with arterio-graphically proven single-vessel coronary artery obstructions, and from patients with arterio-graphically proven normal coronary arteries and normal ventricular function. T1-201 scintigraphs were collected after maximal exercise from the 78 kV photopeak with a 20% window, using a portable gamma camera equipped with a 1/4-inch crystal and high-resolution collimator. Three views of the left ventricle—anterior (ANT), left lateral (LAT), and left lateral anterior oblique (LAO)—required approximately 10 minutes with a minimum of 300,000 scintillation counts collected in each view [Cios et. al., 1991]. The scintigraphs were then processed by comparing the normalized count ratio for each pixel at a given anatomic location with that obtained previously from a group of subjects having normal myocardial perfusion. Pixels containing count ratios that fell more than 2.5 standard deviations below normal were considered to be under-perfused. Each of the three views was divided into 10 anatomic regions called "segments." For computer analysis, the segments of all three views were numbered consecutively (see Figure 4.1) [Cios et. al., 1991]. Segments 1 through 10 of the left lateral view are referred to as regions 11 through 20, and segments 1 through 10 of the left anterior oblique view are referred to as regions 21 through 30. The percentage of under-perfused (as compared with normally perfused) pixels in each region represents the magnitude of the perfusion defect for that region. Thus, 30 numbers ranging in size from 0 to 100, each representing the size of the perfusion defect in that region, were generated from each patient scintigraph.

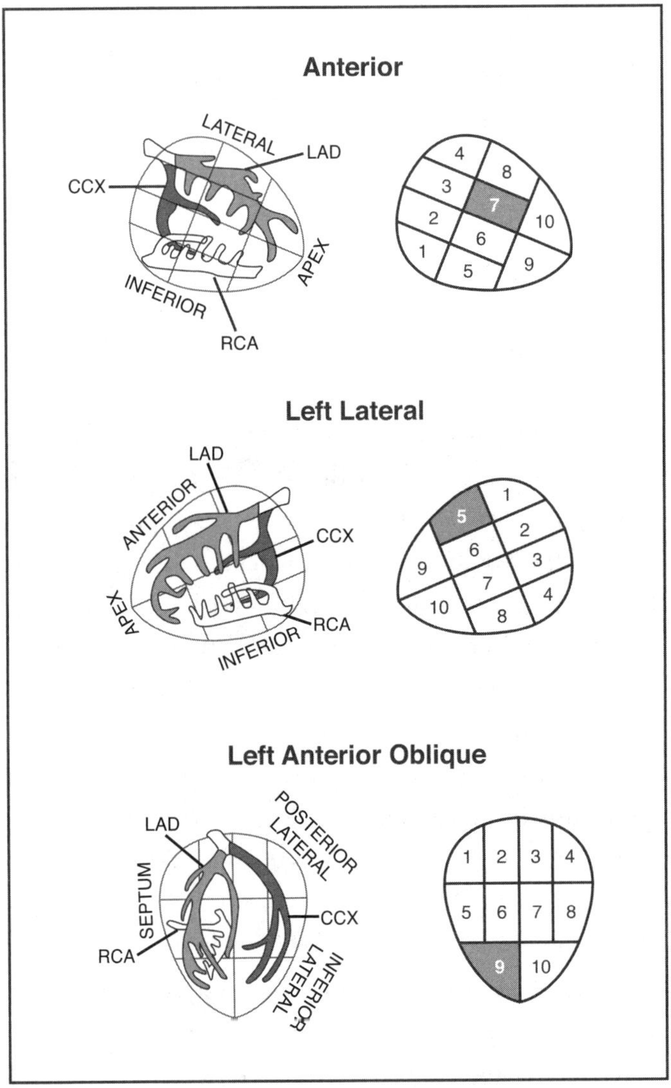

Figure 4.1 Three views of a scan and the numbering scheme for the segments of each view: CCX stands for circumflex artery, LAD for left anterior descending artery, and RCA for right coronary artery [Cios et. al., 1991].

Those 30-dimensional vectors collected from 91 patients, who underwent thallium-201 myocardial scintigraphy, were used as inputs for our hybrid neuro-fuzzy algorithm. Sixty-four scans were chosen at random for training and the remaining 27 scans were used for testing. A significant obstruction was defined as equal to or greater than a 70% narrowing of the main artery. Normal arteries had narrowings of less than 30%. The major coronary arteries were classified as the left anterior descending artery (LAD), right coronary artery (RCA), circumflex artery (CCX), and the posterior descending artery. For data analysis, patients having a significant stenosis upstream from the posterior descending artery were classified as having right coronary artery obstruction, regardless of whether this artery arose from the right coronary or circumflex artery. The training file consisted of 64 thirty-dimensional vectors, which were assigned to the following classes: eight vectors representing patients with CCX, 22 with LAD, 16 with RCA, and 18 normal patients. The testing file consisted of 27 thirty-dimensional vectors—three of them representing CCX, 10 representing LAD, seven representing RCA, and seven representing data collected from normal patients.

Self-generating neural network software was able to correctly classify all the patients, which was an amazing step toward a powerful algorithm for diagnosing coronary artery stenosis from myocardial perfusion scintigraphs, compared with previous attempts that utilized a knowledge-based system with Bayesian methods [Cios et. al., 1989], Dempster-Shafer theory of evidence [Cios et. al., 1990], fuzzy sets with probability assigned membership functions [Cios et. al., 1991], and machine learning algorithms with fuzzy generalized operations [Cios and Sztandera, 1993]. In that work, the authors described a method of aggregating decision rules generated by machine learning algorithms with generalized fuzzy operators. The data were further utilized to derive fuzzy sets representing major coronary artery stenosis using Dombi's operations. Four fuzzy sets were obtained to represent obstructions in three main coronary arteries—namely, left anterior descending (LAD), right coronary artery (RCA), and circumflex (CCX)—and to represent NORMAL patients.

The four sets representing LAD, RCA, CCX, and NORMAL were specified by eight dimensional vectors, since each fuzzy set representing each of the 30 regions was defined using a logarithmic scale dividing a range of possible values of a perfusion defect (0–100) into eight intervals. Furthermore, for each of the four fuzzy sets, an appropriate trapezoidal fuzzy number was derived. Then, linguistic terms—LAD, RCA, CCX, and NORMAL—were assigned to those numbers, respectively. Also, linguistic terms assigned to the trapezoidal fuzzy numbers corresponding to the new patient scintigraphs were derived. Then, the patient linguistic terms were matched with one of the four terms to make a diagnosis.

A similar data set was used in Cios et. al. (1994). It contained 64 patients—46 with stenosis and 18 without. They used trapezoidal membership functions for each of the three scintigraphy views. They evaluated three known learning algorithms: ALFS, CLILP2, and EXP. They formulated 13 different linguistic statements to provide crisp results. The notation used in formulating the if-then statements relates to the medical parameters described in the paper, but one statement is presented here as a demonstration of defuzzification approach:

> "IF LAT4 has perfusion defect value in the range of [0,4], [15,34],[45,54],[85,100] with (0.2) AND LAT8 has perfusion defect value in the range of [5,24],[35,44],[75,100] with (0.4) AND LAT5 has perfusion defect value in the range of [0,4] with (0.4) THEN STENOSIS is in CCX."

They reported on the results of the three different algorithms for defuzzification. Accuracy for classifying normal arteries ranged from 96% to 100%. However, accuracy for correctly classifying stenosis ranged from 85% to 93% for two algorithms. A third had lower accuracy.

In another research approach, Malek et. al. (2009) discussed an automated breast cancer diagnosis system utilizing fuzzy aggregation. They proposed a fuzzy instrument for hardware implementation of the automated system using a CMOS integrated circuit. They reported on active research conducted with 200 patients to prove the concept and finally proposed a concept design for the CMOS integrated circuit.

For the active research, cells were extracted from the patients' lesions and fixed on microscope slides. For each patient, 19 attributes were analyzed. The GVF-Snake model was used to identify the contour of a typical nucleus within the object. Texture-analysis-based feature extraction involved wavelet transforms. Statistical attributes included mean, variance, entropy, and normalized Shannon entropy. The process is mathematically intensive. The fuzzy clustering C-means algorithm, as is available in MATLAB, was used to assign fuzzy set memberships. Each new pattern was assigned a degree of membership of malignant class or benign class. The sum of all membership functions at any point equals 100%. They reported 97% correct classification of benign cases and 93% correct classification of malignant cases.

In yet another approach, Bagher-Ebadian et. al. (2004) used an automated neural network and fuzzy clustering for diagnosis of coronary artery disease. They reported two studies: one with 58 subjects and one with 115. Data was obtained from planar images in three projections—anterior, left anterior oblique, and left lateral—using a collimator. Images were taken at rest and again under stress. Background noise was suppressed by segmenting myocardium from the background using the fuzzy clustering Picard iteration algorithm. Euclidean distance was used as the distance metric.

Each myocardium was partitioned into four sections, and the center of activity was found for each section. Sampling radii were taken every 2 degrees to project the sectors on an x-y plane. There were three transformed projections divided into four regions for "at rest" and the same for "stress." Thus, there were two vectors of dimension 12. The mean and variance row vectors were defined as feature vectors. The number of features was reduced through a selection process based on maximum separation in multidimensional feature space.

The artificial neural network was trained and then evaluated. The true values, normal or abnormal, were obtained from coronary angiographies taken within three months of the imaging. Accuracy in prediction positive results varied from 77% to 86%, and prediction of negative results from 63% to 66%.

An interesting demonstration of fuzzy logic as applied to the more general diagnostic process was presented in Licata (2010). This is different from the previous citations in that it does not deal with data analysis to identify one of two possible outcomes as a "test" for a specific disease. Rather, he suggested that the application of fuzzy set theory in place of the physician's usual reliance solely on probabilistic logic can improve the general diagnosis process, which attempts to identify the cause of observed symptoms.

He developed the fuzzy set theory process through an example application to one case study. Specific symptoms in this case are dyspnea at rest (a), oedema (b), tachyarrhythmias (c), epatomegally (d), ascites (e), and pleural effusion (f). Possible diagnoses would be hepatic cirrhosis (t), nephrosic syndrome (u), pneumonia (w), myocardial ischemia (x) congestive heart failure (y), and worsening of the supraventricular arrhythmias (z).

A typical if-then rule would have the following form:

"If a and b and c and d and e and f, then t or w or x or y or z."

The severity of these symptoms (a, b, c, etc.) is typically linguistic and fuzzy, such as tachyarrhythmias is "slow," "moderate," or "fast."

Numerous laboratory tests provided more data for assignment of fuzzy membership functions. Linguistic observations and laboratory results were assigned set memberships between 0 and 1 through the use of charts that have been prepared.

Defuzzification involves a considerable number of predicate logic statements. These are evaluated using generalized modus ponens, and sometimes more directly. This likely involves a good deal more skill in logic than most physicians would possess. Licata's work points out that the fuzzy logic approach is in lieu of the probabilistic approach generally employed. Licata suggests that the fuzzy set theory solution is more exact and probably superior to the usual process where individual decisions in the chain leading to a conclusion are made on the basis of probabilistic estimates. One case considered serves as an indication of the pervasive influence of fuzzy logic on the medical discipline.

The work presented next offers yet another variation. It employs the normal distribution as set membership functions. These functions are individually adjusted by using weight and varying each standard deviation. Optimization is obtained through the application of a genetic algorithm. Linguistic rules are not employed and hence the fundamental process is applicable to data sets containing many parameters and to classification into more than two categories. The process is applied to several different data sets, and results are compared with the more common statistical regression analysis.

Step 1 of the process involves assigning data to memberships in the fuzzy sets.

Triangular Membership Function

Numerous membership functions are recognized for creating the fuzzy sets [Pedrycz, 1989]. They include triangle, rectangle, parabola, trapezoid, and even projections of one operating characteristic onto another plane. If, for example, an isosceles triangle is used, then the height would generally be considered equal to 1 and the apex is located at the parameter's average value over the totality of past data.

A particular data record will generally have a value for this parameter that is not at the average. Membership will be determined by the height of the line AC in Figure 4.2. This height has a simple relationship shown in the following equations:

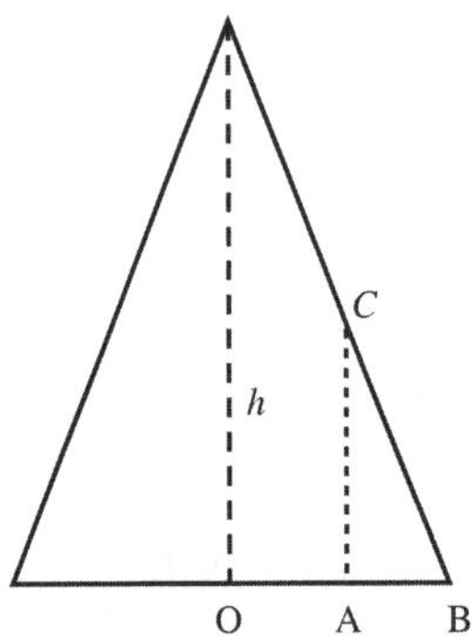

Figure 4.2 Triangular membership function.

$$AC = h \times \frac{AB}{OB} = 1 \times \frac{AB}{OB} = \frac{OB - OA}{OB} = 1 - \frac{OA}{OB}$$

$$\text{Membership} \begin{cases} = 1 - \left|\frac{OA}{OB}\right| & \text{for } |OA| \leq |OB| \\ = 0 & \text{otherwise} \end{cases}$$

It should be noted that the value of O need not be an exact match to the average value of the parameter for all existing data records. In some cases, particularly in cases involving dynamic control systems, the value of O may be designated in accordance with engineering analysis or other considerations.

A comparison of performance with the triangular membership function and the exponential function was reported in Sanford and Sztandera (2010). In this case, some adjustment was made to the triangular base and exponential width in an effort to find the better function. The exponential function performed better in that instance, but triangular, exponential (or sine wave), and trapezoidal are all common.

Trapezoidal Membership Functions

Suppose that there are n generalized fuzzy numbers (A_1, A_2, ..., A_n), with trapezoidal membership functions $A_i = (c_i, a_i, b_i, d_i, w_i)$. The trapezoidal membership function of a generalized fuzzy number, A_i, is then given by the following:

$$\mu_{Ai}(x) = \begin{array}{l} a_i \leq x \leq b_i \\ b_i \leq x \leq c_i \\ c_i \leq x \leq d_i \end{array} \left\{ \begin{array}{l} (x - a_i) / (b_i - a_i) \\ 1 \\ (d_i - x) / (d_i - c_i) \end{array} \right.$$

Exponential Membership Function

Exponential membership functions and sign-wave functions have also been employed. In view of the fact that all parameters in the data sets under study here deal with physical attributes that are most likely normally distributed, the normal distribution suggested itself as a membership function for the current analysis. This distribution is exponential, and probability is measured as between zero and one. The membership function has the convenient property that no parameter will actually have zero membership but will have a diminishingly small membership as its location diverges far from the mean. The probability of being at the mean is ½ and not 1, so for no other reason than esthetics the membership percent was divided by ½ in order to produce membership of 1 for parameters actually at the mean.

The mean for each membership function is the mean of that parameter over existing data. Spread of the membership function is achieved by adjusting the standard deviation. Before training, this value is set at the standard deviation of that parameter over existing data. And membership percentage is determined by the probability of the tail. The following equation describes this:

Membership = P(X)/0.5 for $X \leq \mu$

or

Membership = (1–P(X))/0.5 for $X > \mu$

Thus, for a given parameter such as "thickness":

Standard deviation = σ

Mean = μ

Measured value = x

If $x > \mu$ then membership = (1–P(x))/0.5

If $x < \mu$ then membership = P(x)/0.5

General Aggregation Operations

As noted in Chapter 2, "Computational Intelligence Foundations," aggregation operations are operations by which several fuzzy sets are combined into a single set. In general, any aggregation operation is defined by the mapping [Klir and Yuan, 1995]

$$h:[0,1]^n \rightarrow [0,1]$$

for $n \geq 2$. When applied to n fuzzy sets, A_1, A_2, ...A_n, defined on X, h produces an aggregate fuzzy set, A, by operating on the membership grades, $\mu(x)$ of each $x \in X$ in the aggregated sets. Thus, we have the following:

$$\mu_A(x) = h(\mu_{A1}(x), \mu_{A2}(x), \ldots \mu_{An}(x)) \text{ for each } x \in X$$

The following requirements express the essence of the notion of aggregation, after Klir and Yuan [Klir and Yuan, 1995]:

- **Axiom 1:** h (0, 0, ..., 0) = 0 and h (1, 1, ..., 1) = 1.
- **Axiom 2:** For any pair of numbers a_i, b_i, where $a_i \in [0,1]$, $b_i \in [0, 1]$, if $a_i \geq b_i$ for all i then $h(a_i) \geq h(b_i)$ that is, h is monotonic non-decreasing in all its arguments.

Two additional axioms are also employed to characterize aggregation operations:

- **Axiom 3:** h is a continuous function—that is, it guarantees that an infinitesimal variation in any argument of h does not produce a noticeable change in the aggregate.
- **Axiom 4:** h is a symmetric function in all its arguments—that is, $h(a_i) = h(a_p)$ for any permutation, p, of the arguments. In other words, the aggregated sets are equally important.

Fuzzy unions and intersections can be qualified as aggregation operations on only two arguments; their property of associativity provides a mechanism for extending their definition to any number of arguments. Also, in the case of bisymmetry and strict monotonicity, the extensions are straightforward. Thus, generalized fuzzy unions and intersections can be viewed as special aggregation operations that are symmetric, usually continuous, and are required to satisfy conjunctive and disjunctive attitudes. As a result, generalized fuzzy unions and intersections can produce only aggregates that are subject to the restrictions [Klir and Yuan, 1995]

$$\max(a,b) \leq u(a,b) \leq \mu_{\max}(a,b)$$

and

$$i_{\min}(a,b) \leq i(a,b) \leq \min(a,b)$$

where u(a,b) and i(a, b) are the fuzzy union and the fuzzy intersection, respectively.

Generalized Dombi operations [Dombi, 1982] possess properties of fuzzy unions and intersections, and are utilized here. As noted in Chapter 2, and repeated here for clarity, their membership functions are generated from two formulas.

The following is Dombi's fuzzy union, where λ is a parameter by which different unions are distinguished, and $\lambda \in (0, \infty)$:

$$\frac{1}{1+\left[\left(\frac{1}{a}-1\right)^{-\lambda}+\left(\frac{1}{b}-1\right)^{-\lambda}\right]^{-\frac{1}{\lambda}}}$$

The following is Dombi's fuzzy intersection, where λ is a parameter by which different intersections are distinguished, $\lambda \in (0, \infty)$:

$$\frac{1}{1+\left[\left(\frac{1}{a}-1\right)^{\lambda}+\left(\frac{1}{b}-1\right)^{\lambda}\right]^{\frac{1}{\lambda}}}$$

From the aggregation inequalities, one can see that generalized fuzzy unions and intersections do not produce any aggregates that generate values between min and max. Hence, the general rules previously stated are retained:

- A AND B, where A and B are limited to the range (0, 1), becomes equivalent to min (A, B).
- A OR B, where A and B are limited to the range (0, 1), becomes equivalent to max (A, B).

Aggregates that are not restricted in this way, however, are allowed by Axioms 1 through 4. Operations that produce them are called "averaging operations." There are several classes of averaging operations that are a compromise between min and max. One such class, which covers the entire interval between the min and max operations, consists of generalized means. This class of operations was used in fuzzy prediction, defined after Klir and Yuan (1995) as

$$h_\alpha(a_1, a_2, \ldots a_n) = \left(\frac{a_1^\alpha + a_2^\alpha + \ldots + a_3^\alpha}{n} \right)^{\frac{1}{\alpha}}$$

where α is a parameter by which different means are distinguished, and $\alpha \in R$ (α is not equal to 0). It was set up to 4 based on sample calculations carried out. Function h_α clearly satisfies all axioms of aggregation operations; consequently, it represents a parameterized class of continuous and symmetric aggregation operations.

A variant of this approach is used in the following analysis. The approach uses weighting values for each alpha, and these weighting values may be adjusted for optimum performance. A further variant that is investigated involves multiplication rather than averaging. In that case, the individual weighting factors are of no consequence. Linguistic statements are usually associated with defuzzification. However, in a classification problem when there are many parameters of equal importance, it is difficult to formulate such linguistic statements.

Fuzzy Sets and Data Mining

The typical analytic approach to data mining employs random selection to partition the data into two groups (sometimes three). The first group is used to "train" the data mining algorithm. For example, if regression is employed, the training partition is used to set the parameters used in the regression formula. The usual measures for performance are used for this purpose—residual error, p-values of coefficients, and so on. When two partitions are used, they are usually based on a 60/40 or 70/30 ratio. These are generally accepted ratios, but it's not really possible to demonstrate a theoretical optimum, and if the data set is small, more may be required for training.

Once the data mining model has been selected, it is evaluated against the second partition, usually called the *validation partition*, to see how it performs. If the data has been divided into three partitions, different models may be evaluated against the second data set and small further adjustments may be made to the most promising model before it is evaluated against the third partition of data. Only two partitions were employed for the analysis reported here.

Data in the first partition, "training," are separated into two groups—the first containing data of known benign instances, and the other one containing data of the known malignant instances. For each set, the mean and standard deviation are computed for each of the attributes. These values are then used to set the membership function for each attribute.

When the model is "run," the data from each record is evaluated for membership in each of the two groups of fuzzy sets. The results are aggregated and compared, with the decision for benign or malignant being made on the basis of which aggregation has the larger value. Data from both the first ("training") partition and the second ("validation") partition are evaluated by the model. Usually the training data performs better, as might be expected.

Several aggregation methods have been compared. There is no clear analytical approach for some of the selections. Establishing a data mining model is, in some ways, an empirical process. That is why the methodology using the training partition and the validation partition is usually employed.

The averaging method would be defined as follows. In this case, the individual membership functions are not weighted but the aggregate is.

$\mu_A(x) = \sum_{k=1}^{n} \mu_{Ak}(x_k)$—additive

$\mu_A(x) = \sum_{k=1}^{n} b_k \mu_{Ak}(x_k)$—additive with individual b_k weight adjustment

- μ_A is the membership function for class A.
- μ_{A1} is the membership function for class A, parameter number 1.
- μ_{A2} is the membership function for class A, parameter number 2.
- x_1 is the value of parameter number 1 associated with object x.
- x_2 is the value of parameter number 2 associated with object x.

The aforementioned equations would be repeated for μ_B where A is associated with malignancy and B with benign.

The multiplicative aggregates are defined as follows:

$$\mu_A(x)\prod_{k=1}^{n}\mu_{Ak}(x_k)\text{—multiplicative}$$

$$\mu_A(x) = \prod_{k=1}^{n}(\mu_{Ak}(x_k))^2\text{—multiply squares}$$

In each instance, the individual $\mu_{Ak}(x_k)$ membership functions may be adjusted during the training phase to achieve minimum classification error.

Training

Training is the distinctive feature of the somewhat heuristic model presented here. During the training stage, the standard deviation used in each membership function can be adjusted to improve overall performance of the "training" partition data. Increasing individual standard deviation has the effect of increasing the width of that membership exponential function. The function now departs from the true statistical probability function, but the choice of the normal probability function for the exponential was arbitrary and not usually used in fuzzy logic anyway. The data represent physical attributes, and such attributes might be assumed to have normal distributions. However, the data were obtained from human observations that are quantized, and hence not normal.

The unaided model performed quite well. However, performance was improved by adjusting the value used for standard deviation of each individual parameter associated with each class.

The additive method of combining individual parameter memberships and the product method performed comparably in practice. It would seem that using the squares of membership values would emphasize parameters where there is "good" membership. However, empirical work suggests that there was no significant difference.

An adjusting coefficient may be used when adding membership values. This allows a small amount of improvement in some instances.

With some data-mining models, over-training is possible. In that case, the error percentage is very good for the training partition but markedly degraded for the validation set. This situation did not present itself.

Training Optimization

There are many parameters, and each one has an adjustable standard deviation. Adjusting by heuristics is time consuming. A genetic algorithm was used in an attempt to optimize this process. The genetic algorithm used was a Microsoft Excel add-in called "xl bit" (http://www.xlpert.com) [XLBIT, 2010].

Results with Data Set #1: Statistical Approach

Classification data mining is often accomplished on a statistical basis with a logistic regression model. In order to compare the performance of the fuzzy model, logistic regression was applied to the same data. The vehicle used was a Microsoft Excel add-in called "XLMiner" [XLMiner, 2010].

Results obtained with several data sets are reported here. Data set #1 is "Mammographic Mass Data," made public by Schulz-Wendtland [Elter et. al., 2007]. The mammographic mass database consisted of the following parameters.

- **BI-RADS Assessment**—1 to 5 (ordinal)
- **Age**—Patient's age in years (integer)
- **Shape**—Mass shape: round=1, oval=2, lobular=3, irregular=4 (nominal)
- **Margin**—Mass margin: circumscribed=1, microlobulated=2, obscured=3, ill-defined=4, spiculated=5 (nominal)
- **Density**—Mass density: high=1, iso=2, low=3, fat-containing=4 (ordinal)
- **Severity**—Benign=0 or malignant=1 (binominal)

Missing Attribute Values:

- BI-RADS Assessment	2
- Age	5
- Shape	31
- Margin	48
- Density	76
- Severity	0

The predicted classification is either benign or malignant. Cases with missing variables were removed. A summary of results is in Table 4.1. For these calculations, the gain of each individual fuzzy set was left constant during the aggregation (averaging) process but individual standard deviations were adjusted so as to narrow or increase the width of the membership function. Percentages shown are error percentages. The ratios, such as 7/270, show error count and total records in that classification.

Validation scores are the important ones from the point of view of data analysis. Also, there is not a great deal of variation among results. This seems to match results from some other researchers in this area.

Table 4.1 Summary of Classification Results for Data Set #1

	Benign Errors	Cancer Errors	Overall Error
Logistic Regression (Training)	15.95%	15.61%	15.79%
	41/257	37/237	78/494
Logistic Regression (Validation)	17.96%	15.95%	16.97%
	30/167	26/163	56/330
Fuzzy Logic Model Sum of Membership Values (Training)	19.84%	16.88%	18.4%
	51/257	40/237	91/494
Fuzzy Logic Sum of Membership Values (Validation)	16.17%	17.79%	17.00%
	27/167	29/163	56/330
Fuzzy Logic Model Using Membership Product (Training)	19.46%	16.03%	17.8%
	50/257	38/237	88/494
Fuzzy Logic Model Using Membership Product (Validation)	17.37%	15.95%	16.7%
	29/167	26/163	55/330
Membership Product & Genetic Algorithm to Adjust Sigma (Training)	17.9%	11.39%	14.8%
	46/257	27/237	73/494
Membership Product & Genetic Algorithm to Adjust Sigma (Validation)	20.96%	12.27%	16.7%
	35/167	20/163	55/330
Using Sum of Memberships & Genetic Algorithm to Adjust Sigma (Training)	15.18%	15.61%	15.4%
	39/257	37/237	76/494
Using Sum of Memberships & Genetic Algorithm to Adjust Sigma (Validation)	15.57%	16.56%	16.1%
	26/167	27/163	53/330

Training and validation scores are shown in Table 4.1. As anticipated, training scores are slightly better.

Using the genetic algorithm to optimize the membership functions contributed a slight improvement when the decision rule was based on the sum of membership values and made no improvement in overall accuracy when the product of membership values was used. In this latter instance, it altered the probabilities for failures in detecting malignancy by increasing them with a consequent decrease in failures to classify as benign.

The genetic algorithm, like other training adjustments, worked to minimize the overall error in the training process. The hope is that this will project into improved performance with the validation partition data. It is true that some adjustment of the sigma values in the individual membership functions can be used to shift errors from one type to another while still maintaining overall error rate near constant.

In lieu of adjusting the standard deviations, a weighting factor for each attribute can be adjusted. Of course, this is only possible when the aggregation function is a summation. Thus:

$$\mu_A(x) = \sum_{k=1}^{n} b_k \mu_{Ak}(x_k)$$

The coefficient b_k applies to the attribute k. Results in this simple case are shown in Table 4.2, and they are not markedly different from results previously obtained.

Table 4.2 Summary of Classification Results for Data Set # 1 Using Genetic Algorithm for Optimization

	Benign Errors	Cancer Errors	Overall Error
Sum of Memberships & Genetic Algorithm to Adjust Weight (Training)	13.23% 34/257	20.25% 48/237	16.6% 82/494
Sum of Memberships & Genetic Algorithm to Adjust Weights (Validation)	11.98% 20/167	20.25% 33/163	16.1% 53/330

At least in some instances weighting the membership functions is as useful as adjusting the individual shapes of the membership functions. It is not obvious that this would be the case. It does say that simple dynamic weighting adjustment during the training phase may be as useful as anything else.

Results also suggest that the statistical logistic regression approach is about as valuable as the fuzzy logic approach in this particular approach. This is not the case in control systems where fuzzy logic performs exceedingly well. This example reports on an empirical investigation with a limited amount of data. It offers no proof that statistical methods will always perform as well or less well as fuzzy methods. Not all researchers have reported a comparison, so one hesitates to make generalized observations.

Results Data Set #2

Data set #2 was breast cancer data made public in Mangasarian and Wolberg (1990). This data set was also briefly reported in Sanford and Sztandera (2010). The methodology has now been greatly expanded with adjustment of individual membership functions and use of the genetic algorithm. Data set parameters are as follows:

- **Sample Code Number**: ID number
- **Clump Thickness**: 1–10
- **Uniformity of Cell Size**: 1–10
- **Uniformity of Cell Shape**: 1–10
- **Marginal Adhesion**: 1–10
- **Single Epithelial Cell Size**: 1–10
- **Bare Nuclei**: 1–10
- **Bland Chromatin**: 1–10
- **Normal Nucleoli**: 1–10
- **Mitoses**: 1–10
- **Class**: 2= benign; 4 = malignant

The predicted classification is either benign or malignant. Standard deviation of membership functions was adjusted using the genetic algorithm. Sets were aggregated as an averaging process, and the selection was made on the basis of which was larger. A summary of the results is shown in Table 4.3.

Table 4.3 Summary of Classification Results for Data Set #2

	Benign Errors	Cancer Errors	Overall Error
Logistic Regression (Training)	1.11%	2.88%	1.71%
	3/270	4/139	7/409
Logistic Regression (Validation)	4.02%	3.06%	3.68%
	7/174	3/98	10/272
Using Sum of Memberships & Genetic Algorithm to Adjust Sigma (Training)	4.07%	13.67%	7.3%
	11/270	19/139	30/409
Using Sum of Memberships & Genetic Algorithm to Adjust Sigma (Validation)	1.15%	10.2%	4.4%
	2/174	10/98	12/272

Again, results from the fuzzy approach are very good, and in some respect comparable to statistical logistical regression. Results for data set #2 were considerably better than those for data set #1, possibly because data set #2 had more attributes from which to establish set memberships. All results were really comparable with results of other researchers, as reported earlier.

The fitness chart developed by the genetic algorithm software for data set #2 is presented in Figure 4.3. It shows that the genetic algorithm has approached asymptotically a horizontal line and further iterations may not produce improvement unless there are local minima. However, considering the nature of the problem, local minima are unlikely.

Solution Efficacy

There is naturally a question as to why these analytic attempts are not more successful in discriminating among the two classes. In most medical (and probably most biological) entities, various attributes will be highly correlated. Figure 4.4 presents the correlation matrix for data set #2. Here it can be seen that a high degree of correlation exists. In general, this makes statistical regression less accurate or questionable at least. This limitation will certainly be present in all attempts at discrimination of biological entities until or unless orthogonal characteristics can be found.

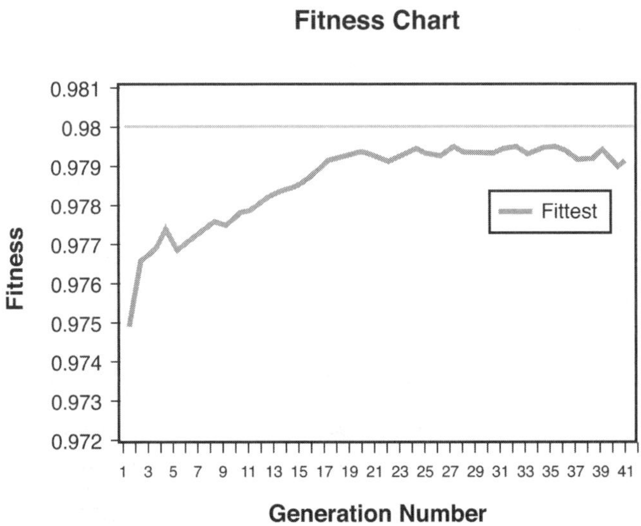

Figure 4.3 Genetic algorithm fitness chart for data set #2.

	Thi	*Uni*	*Sh*	*Ad*	*Siz*	*Nu*	*Ch*	*Nu*	*Mit*	*Cla*
Thick	1.0									
Uniform	0.6	1.0								
Shape	0.7	0.9	1.0							
Adhesion	0.5	0.7	0.7	1.0						
Size	0.5	0.8	0.7	0.6	1.0					
Nuclei	0.6	0.7	0.7	0.7	0.6	1.0				
Chromatin	0.6	0.8	0.7	0.7	0.6	0.7	1.0			
Nucleoli	0.5	0.7	0.7	0.6	0.6	0.6	0.7	1.0		
Mitococ	0.3	0.5	0.4	0.4	0.5	0.3	0.4	0.4	1.0	
Class	0.7	0.8	0.8	0.7	0.7	0.8	0.8	0.7	0.4	1.0

Correlation of Data Set #2

Figure 4.4 Correlation matrix for data set #2.

Observations

Analysis shows that the parameters of data sets are strongly correlated. This is not surprising because they usually represent physical characteristics of some class of objects.

The multiple linear regression model assumes independent variables. Co-linearity may make it impossible to see the contributions of each variable to the result. It can lead to incorrect answers when using regression to fit higher-order polynomials. But this is not a problem here. In the heuristic approach, the model is based on actual performance. No one attempts to say it would be valid for classes different from the ones with which the model is validated.

The fuzzy logic approach presented here is not limited to selection among two categories. Clearly the resolution through a logical OR operation can be applied to multiple categories [Sanford and Sztandera, 2010]. There is no practical limit, provided there is sufficient data. Having three classes requires that training data be divided into three sets; four classes would require four sets, and so on. Statistical evaluation of results would require some reasonable number of records for each class.

Conclusions

It is clear that fuzzy logic employing an exponential membership function, weighted averaging, and a logical OR operation is an effective tool in data analysis involving discrimination where many parameters are involved. It performs as well as results reported by other researchers looking at similar problems with different fuzzy methods and hybrid fuzzy methods. Because membership functions may be adjusted individually, the usual method of dividing data into a training partition and a validation partition is appropriate. Rather extensive adjustment ("learning") during the training stage improves performance. This may include the use of a genetic algorithm. Results observed here corroborate the previous findings; however, only two data sets were used. From these observations it appears that fuzzy logic is comparable but does not always outperform usual data analysis methods such as logistic regression. In instances where image analysis is a principal feature (as reported earlier), the situation does not lend itself to standard statistical regression methods.

4.3 Extracting Information from Failure Equipment Notifications: Use of Fuzzy Sets to Determine Optimal Inventory

4.3.1 Introduction

This section addresses the use of a data analysis approach to extract information from a large number of failure equipment notifications. Based on that, a fuzzy system, capable of learning and optimizing the knowledge from historical evidence, is formed. Subsequently, its use as a guiding tool in decision-making processes at the strategic level (estimation of the number of spare parts based on the warehouse location and type of failure) is outlined. To highlight its advantages, the fuzzy sets approach for spare parts allocation is compared with a probabilistic one [Sztandera, 2011].

Many businesses purchase expensive computer equipment to carry out their services. The computer equipment suppliers that sell these complex systems not only supply the businesses with the product, but must also ensure that the systems remain constantly functional.

However, computer equipment systems invariably fail, generating a demand for repair parts. This demand is extremely time sensitive, as the computer equipment systems, and the businesses that depend on these systems, become crippled without the timely response of a repair vendor with the appropriate service parts. The consequences in the event of equipment failure or malfunction could cause significant losses to the company.

Policies regarding where and how many repair parts to store are far from obvious. For example, storing many and different types of repair parts close to the businesses' locations will virtually guarantee an extremely rapid response to a failure.

However, a computer equipment company would hardly be able to economically justify such a policy due to the cost of maintaining many warehouses, and of holding a generous number of repairable parts in inventory. In the latter case, holding parts "in storage" causes the computer equipment company to incur an opportunity cost, primarily a function of the company's inability to derive revenue—either directly from the sale of the repair part or indirectly through the part's inherent value—while the part sits in a warehouse unused (potentially becoming obsolete) [Schroeder and Gibson, 2007].

4.3.2 Use of Fuzzy Sets to Determine Optimal Inventory

Fuzzy sets incorporate a simple, rule-based IF X AND Y THEN Z approach to solving a control problem rather than attempting to model a system mathematically. The fuzzy sets model is empirically based, relying on an operator's experience rather than their technical understanding of the system. For example, rather than dealing with numerical values in the measured attributes, terms such as "IF (input 1 is adjective 3) AND (input 2 is adjective 3) THEN (output is adjective 2)" and "IF (input 2 is adjective 2) AND (input 4 is adjective 1) AND (input 5 is adjective 5) THEN (output is adjective 6)" are used. These terms are imprecise and yet very descriptive of what must actually happen. Fuzzy sets are capable of mimicking this type of behavior at a very high rate.

Fuzzy set approach requires some numerical parameters in order to operate, such as what is considered a significant error and a significant rate-of-change error, but exact values of these numbers are usually not critical unless very responsive performance is required, in which case empirical tuning would determine them.

The fuzzy sets approach was conceived as a better method for sorting and handling data, but has proven to be an excellent choice for many system applications because it mimics human logic. It can be built into anything, from small handheld products to large computerized process-control systems. It uses an imprecise but very descriptive language to deal with input data, more like a human operator. It is very robust and forgiving of operator and data input and often works when first implemented with little or no tuning.

Spare Parts Stock Level Calculations: Item Approach

In order to appreciate the advantages of the fuzzy rule–based approach, we will first step through a set of examples detailed by Fukuda [Fukuda, 2008] using the Poisson probability process. The purpose of the spare computer parts stock level calculations – item approach is to describe a technique to calculate the spare parts quantity (for a given computer cluster size and inventory), taking into account item reliability (which can be initially modeled by the Poisson probability process).

Variables considered in this approach, after Fukuda (2008), were as follows:

1. Reliability of the item to be a spare, expressed as failure, removal, or replacement, or inversely as mean time between removals (MTBR) in usage hours.
2. Number of items installed per machine (indicated as A).
3. Required probability that a spare will be available when needed—that is, the chance of having a spare part in inventory when required (90% ≤ P ≤ 95%), also called Fill Rate or confidence level.

4. Number of machines to be supported (N).
5. Period to be supported as operational time or between initial and subsequent order (time T in months).
6. Average machine utilization (M in hours per month or day per machine). It may be expressed in % (e.g., 9.5 h/day = 9.5 h/24h = 39.58%).

   Spare parts are divided, for application of this approach, into repairable and nonrepairable. For repairable parts, a stock level of spare parts was calculated to compensate items undergoing the process of repair.
7. For repairable items, an average time it takes to repair (indicated as time between repairs, RT) was considered instead of time of support (T) from point 5. Also, it is advisable to take into account an additional stock level of spare parts to compensate for unavoidable scrap of some repairable items.
8. The scrap rate of a repairable item can be estimated from historical evidence (e.g., R = 0.15 or 1.5%).

Poisson distribution can be used in spare parts quantity determination as a forecasting technique with the use of reliability analysis [Fukuda, 2008]. The demand for spare parts for covering replacement of failed items, occurring as a result of maintenance action, is an event described as the Poisson distribution process, assuming it occurs at a constant average rate and the number of events occurring in any interval is independent of the number of events occurring in any other time interval. These rather strict requirements are replaced in the fuzzy systems approach.

$$f(x;\lambda,t) = \frac{(\lambda t)^{x} e^{-\lambda t}}{x!}$$

- λ is the failure rate.
- t is time (or total operational period of all items).

- x is the number of failures (or number of spare parts required).
- λt is the mean value (number of failures in time t)

In terms of the probability of n or fewer failures in time t, we have the following [Fukuda, 2008]:

$$R(t) = \sum_{x=0}^{n} \frac{(\lambda t)^{x} e^{-\lambda t}}{x!} = e^{-\lambda t}\left[1 + \lambda t + \ldots\ldots\ldots + \frac{(\lambda t)^{n}}{n!}\right]$$

Nonrepairable Items

After Fukuda (2008), for these items the number of failures is equal to the number of spare parts. The quantity of spare parts is the minimum value of n that satisfies the following condition as close as possible:

$$P \leq \sum_{x=0}^{n} \frac{(\lambda t)^{x} e^{-\lambda t}}{x!} = e^{-\lambda t}\left[1 + \lambda t + \ldots\ldots\ldots + \frac{(\lambda t)^{n}}{n!}\right]$$

Here, t is a total operating time for all items. Thus, attributing to Fukuda (2008), the number of failures in time t can be expressed as follows:

$$\lambda t = \frac{1}{\text{MTBR}} t = \frac{\text{AxNxMxT}}{\text{MTBR}} = \frac{\text{AxNxM}}{\text{MTBR}} T$$

It is worth noting [Fukuda, 2008] that the preceding equation can be also directly used as a deterministic method for computing spare parts quantity. T may be mean resupply time, order, or production lead time.

Numerical Example (Nonrepairable Items)

Following Fukuda (2008), let's calculate the spare parts quantity of a nonrepairable item that is installed on four units per machine (A = 4EA) and having a mean time between removals of 7,500 usage hours (MTBR = 7,500 h) for a computer cluster of two machines (N = 2), operating each one for 225 usage hours per month (M = 225 h/month/machine) and considering an initial period of 2 years (T = 24 months) to achieve a confidence level of 90% (P = 0.90).

$$\frac{AxNxMxT}{MTBR} = \frac{(4EA)x(2ac)x(225FH/ac/month)x(24month)}{7.500FH} = 5.76EA$$

Proceeding recursively, we have the following:

- For zero spare parts, P = exp (-5.76) = 0.003 = 0.3% < 90%.
- For one spare part, P = 0.003(1+5.76) = 0.02 = 2% < 90%.
- For two spare parts, P = 0.003(6.76+16.6) = 0.07 = 7% < 90%.
- For three spare parts, P = 0.003(23.36+31.85) = 0.17 = 17% < 90%.
- For four spare parts, P = 0.003(55.21+45.9) = 0.303 = 30.3% < 90%.
- For five spare parts, P = 0.003(101.1+52.8) = 0.462 = 46.2% < 90%.
- For six spare parts, P = 0.003(153.91+50.7) = 0.614 = 61.4% < 90%.
- For seven spare parts, P = 0.003(204.6+41.7) = 0.74 = 74% < 90%.
- For eight spare parts, P = 0.003(246.3+30.1) = 0.83 = 83% < 90%.
- For nine spare parts, P = 0.003(276.4+34.2) = 0.932 = 93.2% > 90%.

We thus obtain the recommended quantity of nine spare parts, which could be used in our decision-making process at the tactical level (optimal inventory of nonrepairable spare parts at a given warehouse).

Repairable Items

For these items, the number of failures is different from the number of spare parts. As indicated in Fukuda (2008), it is a direct application of Palm's theorem. The stock level of spare parts has to compensate for repairable items undergoing the process of repair and could be expressed by the following [Fukuda, 2008]:

$$\lambda t = \frac{1}{\text{MTBR}} = \frac{\text{AxNxMxRT}}{\text{MTBR}} = \frac{\text{AxNxM}}{\text{MTBR}}\text{RT}$$

To replace the very first failed item, it is necessary to have an initial single spare part. Thus, substituting n with (n–1) in the non-repairable parts equation, we obtain the following:

$$P \le \sum_{x=0}^{n-1} \frac{(\lambda t)^x e^{-\lambda t}}{x!} = e^{-\lambda t}\left[1 + \lambda t + \ldots\ldots\ldots \frac{(\lambda t)^{n-1}}{(n-1)!}\right]$$

Numerical Example (Repairable Items)

As pointed out in Fukuda (2008), considering the example of nonrepairable items, we can calculate the number of spare repairable parts taking into account a repair time of 3 months (RT = 3 months) [Fukuda, 2008]:

- For zero spare parts, P = exp(-0.72) = 0.487 = 48.7% < 90%.
- For one spare part, P = 0.487(1+0.72) = 0.837 = 83.7% < 90%.
- For two spare parts, P = 0.487(1.72+0.259) = 0.963 = 96.3% > 90%.

We thus obtain the recommended quantity of (n–1) = 2 or n = 3 spare parts, which could be used again in our decision-making process at the tactical level (optimal inventory of repairable spare parts at a given warehouse).

Repairable Items with Scrap Rate

Repairable items returned to the shop are sometimes scrapped (that is, not repaired) because through inspection, it is decided that some items were not economically feasible to repair. The scrap generally results in an increase of spare parts requirement. For this scenario, the approach could be a combination of repairable and nonrepairable methods [Fukuda, 2008].

Numerical Example (Scrap Rate)

Let's calculate the number of spare parts, if an item is considered a repairable with scrap rate of 10% (R = 0.10).

Previously (from the nonrepairable item numerical example), we had nine failures in the period requiring maintenance, thus $0.1 \times 9 \sim 1$ EA becomes scrap. From the repairable item numerical example, the total number of parts to support the operation was 3 EA. Adding 1 EA discarded now results in four spare parts [Fukuda, 2008].

Note

The previously described *item* approaches can be extended to *system* approaches, where the objective would be to solve the system maintenance problem in determining the maximum total fill rate, or alternatively the minimum total expected backorder in terms of repairable spare parts given a specific amount of allocated funds.

Fuzzy Rule–based System

The probability approach [Fukuda, 2008], as outlined earlier, requires that an event be described as a Poisson distribution process, assuming it occurs at a constant average rate and the number of events occurring in any interval is independent of the number of events occurring in any other time interval. Thus, this research was focused on deriving an optimized fuzzy rule-based system from real-life failure data, where those strict requirements are relaxed. Such a system would be a great asset to any decision maker dealing with the estimation of the number of spare parts based on the warehouse location and type of failure (strategic decisions).

The data used in the analysis came as a courtesy of Prof. Garth Gibson, the Computer Science Department at Carnegie Mellon University and its Computer Failure Data Repository (CFDR) [Gibson and Schroeder, 2009]. It was acknowledged that with the growing scale of today's IT installations, component failure was becoming a significant problem. Yet, very little data on failures in real systems were publicly available, forcing researchers working on system reliability to base their work on simulated rather than empirical data.

The Computer Failure Data Repository (CFDR) [Gibson and Schroeder, 2009] aims at accelerating research on system reliability by providing a collection of public data with detailed failure from a variety of large production systems.

In the reported research, memory hardware failure data collected on a 212-node server farm at Internet services cluster Ask.com, from December 2006 through February 2007, were used. The data themselves were collected by the University of Rochester researchers who contributed to the repository [Li et. al., 2007]. The set consisted of 1,698 seven-dimensional vectors. The dimensions were as follows:

- **Machine ID**—Generic machine name
- **First seen**—When the error was first observed
- **Last seen**—When the error was last observed
- **Times**—How many times the error in that error correction code (ECC) word was reported during the whole monitoring period

- **Address**—The system address of the error (that is, physical memory address)
- **Row/Column/Bank**—The row/column/bank address of the error, translated from the system address
- **Syndrome**—Error syndrome, which can be used to determine which bits are wrong within an ECC word

---

Note

ECC (error correction code) allows data that are being read or transmitted to be checked for errors.

Dimensionality Reduction

Dimensionality reduction techniques (data analysis algorithms) were employed to identify the most contributing dimensions from the set [Sztandera, 2009].

One of the approaches used was regression analysis, and it is highlighted next. Yet another approach could be a count of the repeating fuzzy rules to determine the retained ones.

Though all the independent attributes contribute in the regression equation toward estimation of the number of spare parts, some of the attributes contribute more than others. If the attributes that contribute the least to the prediction ability of the regression equation are eliminated, the overall dimensionality of the data set comes down. Using stepwise regression analysis, one can reduce the dimensionality of the data, keeping only the most influential properties while eliminating properties that contribute minimally to the prediction ability of the regression equation. In addition to using Beta standardized coefficients as indicators while determining the importance of each attribute in the regression equation, partial correlation coefficients can also be used as indicators because they are measures of association between an attribute and the number of spare parts when the influences of the rest of the attributes are removed. Similar to the Beta coefficients, their absolute magnitudes reflect their relative degree of association with estimation of the number of spare parts. The absolute magnitude of partial coefficient ranges from 0 to 1. A partial correlation coefficient with a value close to 1 is an indication that the attribute is strongly associated with the number of spare parts, and the opposite is true for partial correlation coefficients with values close to 0.

It was found out that the most important features were location (machine ID), error type (error syndrome), and count (how many times the error in that error correction code word was reported during the whole monitoring period).

Generation of Fuzzy Rules

Subsequently, a fuzzy rule generation algorithm was used to generate a knowledge base for decision-making processes. A correlation analysis approach (as opposed to data point rules) was used to come up with an optimized knowledge base. In practical terms it means clipping rule-consequent fuzzy sets by the degree of truth of the rule's antecedent.

Thus, instead of generating an impractical set of 1,698 rules, the system came up with an optimized knowledge base with 12 rules that could be used in the decision-making processes at the strategic level (estimation of the number of spare parts based on the warehouse location and type of failure). The obtained knowledge base is listed here.

Fuzzy rules (optimized):

- IF location IS location_M1 AND error IS error_type_0x0 THEN count IS around_6;
- IF location IS location_M1 AND error IS error_type_0x1 THEN count IS around_60;

- IF location IS location_M1 AND error IS error_type_0x2 THEN count IS around_3;
- IF location IS location_M1 AND error IS error_type_0x3 THEN count IS around_50;
- IF location IS location_M6 AND error IS error_type_0x0 THEN count IS around_3;
- IF location IS location_M6 AND error IS error_type_0x1 THEN count IS around_1;
- IF location IS location_M6 AND error IS error_type_0x2 THEN count IS around_3;
- IF location IS location_M6 AND error IS error_type_0x3 THEN count IS around_3;
- IF location IS location_M8 AND error IS error_type_0x0 THEN count IS around_1;
- IF location IS location_M8 AND error IS error_type_0x1 THEN count IS around_3;
- IF location IS location_M8 AND error IS error_type_0x2 THEN count IS around_1;
- IF location IS location_M8 AND error IS error_type_0x3 THEN count IS around_1;

Conclusions

Because repair parts can be extremely valuable, even minor reductions in the inventory of repair parts can result in significant savings for the computer equipment company. Therefore, research investigating optimal inventory policies is important. In addition to determining the stocking levels for each part at each warehouse, questions concerning the number and location of warehouses must also be answered. Different types of warehouses must be considered. Some only hold inventory, whereas others hold inventory and repair broken parts.

A final level of complexity presents itself in determining the way in which warehouses interact—for example, whether one warehouse ships parts to another stocked-out warehouse [Sztandera, 2010, 2011].

4.4 The Use of Computational Intelligence in the Design of Polymers and in Property Prediction

4.4.1 Introduction

Quantitative structure property relationships (QSPRs) are (generally linear) relationships that are used to correlate the structure of compounds with their physical or molecular properties. These types of relationships show considerable potential in a wide range of scientific areas, including thermodynamics, computational drug design, and material science. Within the last of these areas, material science, the formulation of a new polymer with desired properties usually involves a laborious and expensive trial-and-error procedure, but this may largely be avoided using computer search techniques. Computational intelligence (CI) based methods [Cartwright, 1994], which we consider here, are increasingly used, and their use can avoid a subtle disadvantage of traditional approaches; this is that in the latter the choice of candidate molecules is within the control of the researcher, which can prejudice the nature of the modifications that candidate molecules suffer. Should the optimum polymer formulation exist in an unexpected region of search space, that ideal solution will never be located if the researcher believes investigation of that region will be fruitless. CI methods operate without this sort of bias.

Research reported here is based on Chen et. al (2012). Two techniques of computational intelligence are utilized: artificial neural networks (ANNs) and genetic algorithms (GAs) [Curteanu and Cartwright, 2011]. The role of an artificial neural network in the first application outlined here is to solve the "forward problem," which is the prediction of the properties of a polymer, given its molecular structure. A genetic algorithm is used then to solve the "backward problem"—that is, designing the structure of a novel polymer whose properties match as closely as possible those in a list of desirable properties. Various factors in addition to the molecular structure may affect the properties of a finished polymeric product, so the problem is approached first as one of monomer design, and then expanded to include polymerization process conditions, fiber spinning, yarns, and fabrics. Reported here are some results from the ANN approach, and also from a further study in which a combined ANN-GA algorithm is used to investigate polymer properties [Chen et. al., 2008; Curteanu and Cartwright, 2011].

Polymer Design

Polymers offer considerable potential as the base material for cost-effective optical components, such as optical fibers and lenses. If polymer-based products are to be commercially attractive as optical transmission components, it is essential that the polymers be easy to manipulate and sufficiently robust that they can tolerate rough handling during installation; they must also, of course, possess the required optical properties and reliability. The focus here is on one of the parameters that can influence the properties of polymer optical fibers, the glass transition temperature, T_g. Ballato suggested that performance can be optimized by engineering a polymer that exhibits a lower refractive index and T_g [Ballato et. al., 2001].

Numerous attempts have been made to correlate T_g with polymer structure, including the construction of a variety of group contribution and empirical or semi-empirical models. In Van Krevelen (1990), for example, a group contribution approach was used to calculate values not only for the glass transition temperature, but also for other physical and mechanical properties. Following on from Van Krevelen's work, further empirical correlations have been developed. Zuniga and Trevino (2003) devised a simpler group contribution scheme to predict T_g. They calculated 66 contribution values of relatively small groups in an approach that was more flexible than that used by Van Krevelen.

In a new group contribution method, Marrero and Gani (2001) divided chemical groups into three levels. The first included the simple functional groups required to describe a wide variety of compounds, while the second and third levels included poly-functional and structural groups carrying information that was not contained in the first order groups. The main shortcoming of such group contribution methods is that they are applicable only when the group contribution values for the polymers are known in advance. A secondary disadvantage is that their predictions of T_g tend to be related only weakly to the position of functional groups, as opposed to the identity of the groups. Consequently, the properties of isomeric polymers that contain the same functional groups but with different geometry are usually predicted to be very similar.

This section describes how an artificial neural network approach has been employed to attack the glass transition temperature prediction problem. In order to obtain an effective network, descriptors that physical and chemical considerations suggest can be expected to be of relevance were selected by combining the computational intelligence methods mentioned earlier. Contribution information was collected without requiring explicit values for each contribution, thus avoiding the limitation that restricts the applicability of group contribution methods. Descriptors that relate to chemical bonding and to intermolecular bonding were included.

Glass Transition Temperature Database

A database of 71 polymers, represented by their repeating units, was compiled. Experimental data for polymer glass transition temperatures were taken from Van Krevelen (1990), Zuniga and Trevino (2003), Katritzky et. al. (1998), and suppliers' datasheets. Polymers have a high molecular weight because they contain many monomeric units, so the influence of the pair of end-cap groups is expected to be slight; these groups were therefore neglected in the calculations. Twenty-one polymers were selected at random from the database for prediction testing, and the remaining 50 polymers were used for network training.

The structure of each polymer was described by its constituent groups in both the main and the side chain. A linear correlation of T_g and constituent groups was developed by multiple linear regression analysis, expressed by the following equation:

$$T_g = \frac{\sum Y_i N_i}{\sum M_i N_i} + \text{constant}$$

In this equation, Y_i is the contribution of group *i* to the glass transition temperature, N_i is the number of group *i* in the repeating unit, and M_i is the molecular weight of group *i*. The value of T_g calculated from this equation was used as one of the descriptors in the development of a model with 10 descriptors.

As reported in Chen et. al. (2008), Cao and Lin found that it was the size of the terminal group (R_{ter}) in the side chain rather than the total size of that chain that correlates with the glass transition temperature of polymers, when other factors are excluded. Therefore, two descriptors of the volume of the terminal group in the side chain, $MV(R_{ter})$, and the free length of the side chain (L_F) were introduced to study how the geometry of the side chain affected T_g. Individual and intermolecular bond energies were also considered.

The Free Energy change on melting is related to the mobility of the polymer chain and the intermolecular forces that exist between the chains. The main chain bond was recorded as the type of bond, such as C – C, C – O, or C – N, in the backbone of the polymer. Hydrogen bonding is the strongest type of intermolecular bond and, when present, may substantially increase T_g. In the database the number of hydrogen bonds, the hydrogen bond energy, and the density of hydrogen bonds were recorded. Nylon is a notable example of the influence of hydrogen bond density on T_g. In naming Nylons, the number after the name is the number of carbon atoms between two nitrogen atoms, which can participate in the formation of hydrogen bonds. As this number increases, the hydrogen bond density decreases, and T_g also decreases, from around 398K for Nylon 6 to roughly 310K for Nylon 12. In the database, aromatic rings in repeating units were recorded as hydrogen bond acceptors and treated as a participant in a hydrogen bond. The density of hydrogen bonds in the database could then be expressed as follows:

$$\text{Density} = \frac{\text{min(no. of hydrogen bonding donor, no. of hydrogen bonding acceptor)}}{\text{no. of atoms in main chain}}$$

Model Development

A model was formed using a back propagation artificial neural network. Twenty-eight descriptors were classified into three groups: polymer structure descriptors, main chain bond descriptors, and hydrogen bond descriptors. The goal was to find models that required a small number of descriptors, yet generated high R^2 values, in this way identifying the descriptors that are most strongly linked to T_g. This goal was found to be best met by replacing the constituent group descriptors with the pre-calculated T_g, thus reducing the number of descriptors to 10. This reduction in the total number of descriptors not only leads to a marginal improvement in processing speed, but can also lead to a more robust network.

As an alternative to the empirical approach described here, Principal Component Analysis (PCA) can also be used as an identification tool (see Figure 4.5) to pick out key descriptors. In this approach, the set of descriptors is transformed mathematically from a space in which some descriptors may be correlated, or even redundant, into a new space in which a smaller number of orthogonal, and therefore uncorrelated, vectors exist. If several descriptors are found grouped together after the transformation, they can be replaced by a single new descriptor that accounts for all the variability in the descriptors that have been replaced. The use of PCA to reduce the size of a descriptor set is widespread, especially when the set that forms the starting point for an analysis is large (perhaps as many as several hundred). In the reported study the number of starting descriptors is much smaller, so the PCA approach is not essential.

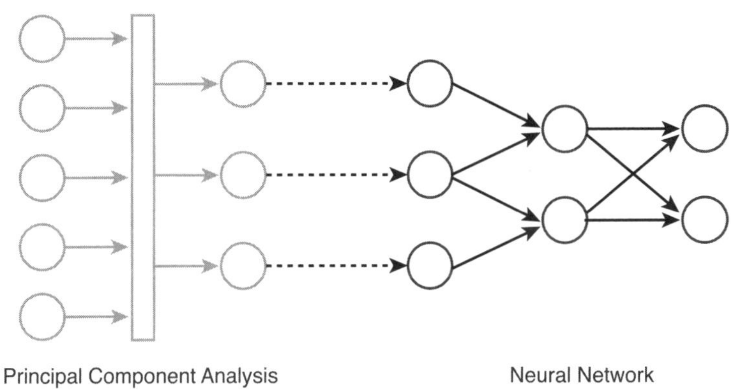

Figure 4.5 Preliminary reduction of a descriptor set using Principal Component Analysis.

Results: Group Contributions Model

A set of randomly selected test polymers was studied. From the database of 71 polymers, 21 polymers (30%) were selected at random to test the predictability of the neural network trained by the remaining 50 polymers. Two separate models were developed in the case study, one with 28 descriptors and a second with 10 descriptors. R^2

values for predictions were as follows: for 28 descriptors R^2 = 0.89, and for 10 descriptors R^2 = 0.85.

Glass Transition Temperatures for Terpolymers

Related studies have also investigated the use of ANNs to predict T_g for a series of terpolymers synthesized from varying ratios of the monomers n-octadecyl acrylate, ethyl acrylate, and acrylonitrile. T_g for materials formed by co-polymerisation of these monomers varies significantly with composition, and shows a nonlinear correlation with mole fraction, covering a range of 232.9K to 343.9K for the polymers in the terpolymer database. Input to the ANN comprised composition of the polymer by mole fraction, while output was the calculated glass transition temperature.

Results: Glass Transition Temperatures for Terpolymers

A neural network working with this database initially showed little sign of learning. As Figure 4.6 indicates, a negligible reduction in training error was evident over 500 epochs; in addition, during this period the network output showed almost no correlation with the desired output. Investigation showed that during this phase of training a scaling of the inputs by the neural network's connection weights was taking place. Once this scaling was largely complete, at around 600 epochs, learning commenced, leading to the creation of a neural network capable of effectively predicting T_g values from terpolymer composition.

A typical set of results is shown in Table 4.4, in which it is evident that the agreement between experimental and predicted glass transition temperatures is generally good.

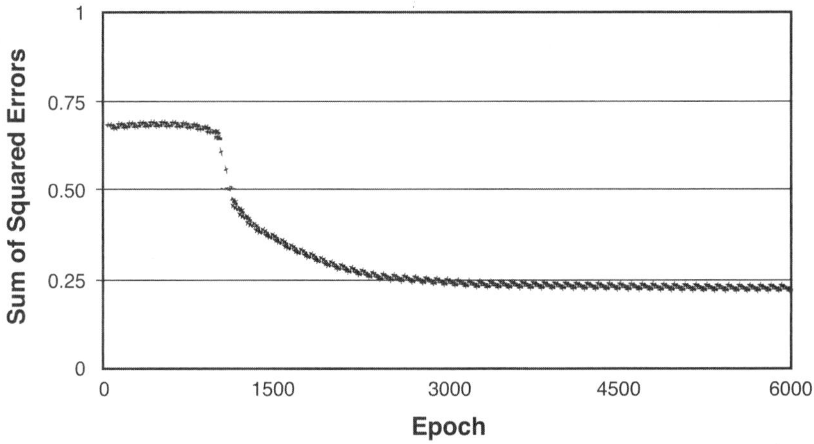

Figure 4.6 Variation of network error with epoch.

Table 4.4 Experimental and Predicted Glass Transition Temperatures

Experimental T_g	Predicted T_g
343.9	319.1
307.9	311.6
301.9	297.2
299.9	316.6
295.9	310.3
309.9	292.2
269.9	270.9
312.9	310.9
285.9	296.2
265.9	272.4
300.9	303.3
276.9	281.8
257.9	260.6
253.9	254.3
289.9	290.4
269.9	268.9
237.9	253.5

Experimental T_g	Predicted T_g
256.5	250.1
251.9	244.8
270.2	271.2
285.9	283.6
285.5	282.8
264.9	263.5
244.9	253.4
237.9	248.9
234.9	237.6
279.9	277.6
259.9	260.6
274.9	251.0
232.9	242.6
244.9	272.2
279.9	271.1
269.9	269.8
239.9	236.2
266.9	267.5
277.9	273.2
280.9	271.3
267.4	271.1
277.9	271.1

The reverse process (in other words, using T_g as the sole input to an ANN and requiring prediction of the composition of the polymer) is considerably harder. This is because the inverse relationship between composition and T_g is not unique: a polymer of specified composition can have only one transition temperature, but by contrast one particular transition temperature may be associated with several polymers of different composition. To investigate the extent to which it might be possible to use T_g values to determine polymer composition, a combined ANN-GA model has been used—with the transition temperature as the sole input, and the terpolymer composition as output. The role of the GA here is to optimize the neural network's architecture (the number of hidden layers and the number of nodes within those layers) and the adjustable parameters that govern network learning, including the learning rate and the type of activation function [Curteanu and Cartwright, 2011]. The error in the prediction of fractional composition is given by the following equation:

$$E = \sum_{k} (\text{prediction}_k - \text{target}_k)^2$$

Some typical results appear in Table 4.5.

Table 4.5 Polymer Composition Predicted from Glass Transition Temperature

N-octadecyl Acrylate Fraction	Ethyl Acrylate Fraction	Acrylonitrile Fraction	Error
0.726	0.050	0.223	1.007
0.304	0.664	0.031	1.292
0.326	0.061	0.611	0.175
0.603	0.013	0.383	0.606
0.514	0.160	0.325	0.563
0.404	0.220	0.375	0.387
0.288	0.205	0.505	0.188
0.159	0.364	0.476	0.122
0.652	0.014	0.333	0.603
0.452	0.274	0.272	0.384
0.098	0.624	0.276	0.240
0.179	0.458	0.361	0.154
0.079	0.479	0.441	0.086
0.059	0.284	0.655	0.009
0.363	0.376	0.259	0.213
0.451	0.213	0.335	0.245
0.367	0.351	0.281	0.118
0.378	0.193	0.428	0.084
0.147	0.373	0.479	0.010
0.483	0.287	0.229	0.122
0.033	0.489	0.476	0.031

N-octadecyl Acrylate Fraction	Ethyl Acrylate Fraction	Acrylonitrile Fraction	Error
0.112	0.577	0.310	0.033
0.177	0.113	0.708	0.213
0.288	0.210	0.501	0.088
0.295	0.383	0.321	0.045
0.455	0.464	0.079	0.232
0.183	0.327	0.489	0.118
0.064	0.446	0.489	0.013
0.045	0.512	0.442	0.005
0.051	0.135	0.812	0.259
0.494	0.135	0.369	0.158
0.222	0.295	0.482	0.012
0.372	0.132	0.494	0.489
0.709	0.208	0.081	0.574
0.215	0.753	0.031	0.129
0.246	0.554	0.199	0.023
0.501	0.093	0.405	0.290
0.071	0.250	0.677	0.207
0.716	0.115	0.167	0.351
0.137	0.421	0.440	0.045

As the table shows, the glass transition temperature is adequately predicted for a significant proportion of the samples. As argued earlier, it would be unrealistic to expect that the composition of every sample could be predicted correctly from its T_g, no matter what type of model is used. Nevertheless, calculations of this type may be helpful in identifying those materials that have a glass transition temperature that is strongly influenced by composition (and which, therefore, a neural network might reasonably be expected to learn) and other materials that have a T_g that is much less dependent on composition (and for which there is therefore little to guide the network toward the correct composition). In the former case, composition prediction should be accurate and the error low, whereas in the latter case, the error will be high.

Conclusions

Hydrogen bonding is an important factor in determining T_g of polymers. Thus, introducing hydrophilic groups, such as –OH, into a polymer structure should improve both moisture regain and the glass transition temperature. The optical performance of polymer fibers can be adjusted by engineering a polymer exhibiting a lower refractive index and T_g. As recommended by Ballato (2001), it would be beneficial to develop perfluorinated polymers to obtain lower refractive index, because any C-H bonds will lead to increased adsorption. A refractive index can be predicted using the same approach as described here, once refractive index data is included in the ANN training set. The approach used in this study could be used to obtain polymers with both low refractive index and T_g.

It is possible also to use ANNs to establish a direct link between composition and T_g without using group contribution methods. Prediction of T_g from terpolymer composition can be accomplished satisfactorily, whereas the reverse process (determining composition from a single measurement of T_g) is more difficult. Nevertheless, an analysis of the errors in such a calculation may help identify the regions in which T_g is most sensitive to changes in composition and the use of a GA to optimize the ANN for this calculation can reasonably be expected to improve the likelihood of valid predictions.

Exercises

[Level 4] Propose a research project for your M.S. thesis or Ph.D. dissertation that will explore the design and deployment of a sophisticated computational intelligence system to holistically understand business processes at your workplace, and that could be utilized to differentiate your business. Incorporate several existing models to study and communicate the interdependency of the full range of factors and processes. Evaluate different scenarios over long periods of time to allow stakeholders to balance and prioritize trade-offs between the business desire for a higher profit and consumer account for quality and affordability.

5

Future of Computational Intelligence

Learning Objectives

- To gain an appreciation for computational intelligence as a powerful tool that allows the best alternatives to emerge (sometimes before reasons for them become apparent) and evolve, and subsequently be leveraged to gain a competitive edge
- To realize that a fundamental shift in organizational culture has been happening, one that radiates from computational intelligence usage and is seen in organizations that have embraced the emerging world of Business Analytics for decision making
- To understand that nowadays computational intelligence drives (and will continue to drive in the future) sustainable competitive differentiation in organizations
- To realize that perhaps rather than the sky, the intelligence is the limit

5.1 Prospects for the Future

Computational intelligence approaches produce outcomes and patterns they extract from multiple data sources. Different approaches produce different perspectives on the nature of these patterns, and their applicability for decision making. No one approach can capture everything. For a particular repository, there is usually an approach that does it best. For very complex big data sets, where we encounter both structured and unstructured data, computational intelligence comes in handy in overcoming the shortcomings of statistical approaches. Different tools, such as artificial neural networks, fuzzy sets, and their fuzzy-neuro hybrids, provide different views of the discovered patterns. When assembled and run through a genetic algorithm, they could evolve and produce the best fit under the circumstances. As the name suggests, genetic algorithms were inspired by the processes observed in natural evolution. They attempt to mimic these processes and utilize them for solving optimization problems under given constraints. Genetic algorithms search through a given set of discovered patterns, modify them if necessary, and produce an offspring as the best alternative with respect to given criteria.

That seems to corroborate statistician George E. P. Box saying that "All models are wrong, but some are useful" [Anderson, 2008]. The models are only approximations, and computational intelligence tackling big data makes it feasible for an algorithm to ask unconventional questions that managers might not consider. This is of paramount importance to innovative businesses.

Computational intelligence can serve as a powerful tool that allows the best alternatives to emerge (sometimes before reasons for them become apparent) and evolve, and subsequently be leveraged to gain a competitive edge.

Those algorithms, artificial neural networks, fuzzy sets, and genetic algorithms, form the basis of computational intelligence. Computational intelligence provides powerful tools for Business Analytics, and it is used by innovative companies, committed to data-driven decision making, to gain insights that inform business decisions. Down the road, it can be used to automate and optimize business processes. Data, information, and subsequently knowledge obtained through Business Analytics are treated as corporate assets (added value) and are leveraged to gain a competitive edge. This opportunity requires a fundamental shift in organizational culture, one that radiates from computational intelligence usage and is seen in organizations that have embraced the emerging world of Business Analytics for decision making.

One possible path of computational intelligence approaches in the future lies along harvesting relevant information from the flow of multimodal data available online. An important part of our information-gathering behavior has always been to find out what others think. With the growing availability and popularity of opinion-rich resources, such as online review sites and blogs, wikis, and mash-ups, new opportunities and challenges arise as businesses now actively use information technologies to seek out and understand the opinions of consumers.

The sudden eruption of activity in the area of opinion mining and sentiment harvesting and analysis, which deals with the computational treatment of opinion, sentiment, and subjectivity in visual, audio, and textual modalities, has thus occurred at least in part as a direct response to the surge of interest in new systems that deal directly with opinions expressed in just a single modality—text. Thus, much of the work to date on subjectivity and sentiment analysis has focused on just textual data.

Given the accelerated growth of social media on the Web, which includes enormous collections of videos (e.g., YouTube), images (e.g., Flickr, Facebook), and audio (e.g., podcasts), the ability to address the identification of opinions and to capture sentiment for diverse modalities has become increasingly important. Computational intelligence makes it feasible to exploit the joint visual, audio, and textual modalities. It is well suited for identifying features relevant to sentiment analysis that could be subsequently used for decision making. It also provides an additional level of granularity to sentiment classification.

The main driving forces behind the development of computational intelligence tools have been the impressive capabilities of biological systems on one hand, and the researchers' desire to create systems with similar capabilities, but adapted to other applications, on the other hand. It was noticed from the outset that computational intelligence systems owed their abilities not only to innovative architectures for processing big data, but to their implementations in hardware as well.

The development of computational intelligence tools to date has mainly emphasized the architectural aspects, with implementation mostly being performed in software that runs on digital computers. But it is clear that computational intelligence will not reach its full potential until data scientists develop hardware that shares most of the properties of a biological system, while retaining the far superior processing speeds of the supercomputer systems today.

Any hardware implementation technology needs to satisfy superior performance criteria in order to serve as a foundation for constructing large scale computational intelligence systems. As such, it has to accommodate a very large number of processing nodes, as the capabilities we ultimately desire to achieve could be found in systems with billions of nodes. Also, any hardware implementation must allow for adaptive learning in terms of forming the connections and their strengths between all the processing units. Such hardware must be as compact as possible and dissipate a manageable amount of power. Perhaps, the hardware at the nanotechnology level could address all the above requirements.

It is also worth noting that existing computational intelligence hardware has been inspired by the design of the brain—that is, it is *neuromorphic* in a sense. However, the operations of the resulting systems only occasionally act *psychomorphic*—that is, working like the mind. Thus, computational intelligence technology must be significantly extended if it is to act like the mind.

Modeling human cognition and consciousness seems to be a great research avenue to explore. There are challenges, though. The self-referential qualities of consciousness place it outside conventional logic upon which scientific models and frameworks have been constructed thus far. Perhaps, computational intelligence, and in particular artificial neural networks' model of brain circuitry, could better deal with features of self-reference. If self-reference was captured as a form of awareness, then it would pave the way for mathematical foundations for a theory of consciousness.

There seems to be no other alternative to the further development of computational intelligence models of ourselves to understand those higher levels of human cognition, including human consciousness.

As noted in the foreword of this book, although the initial revolution in artificial intelligence lost its early momentum, the second revolution in computational intelligence may well avoid the fate of the first. It is not clear to me now how long it will take to completely understand and simulate all the principles of the mind, but it may not be so far away at all.

Exercises

1. Much concern in the business world nowadays centers around innovation and computational intelligence approaches. But even the state that computational intelligence, augmented with cloud and grid computing, as well as social media technologies, might assume in the near future is only the first step in developing cutting-edge decision-making systems. Big data promises automated actionable knowledge creation for both our use and the use of computers. The next step into the future is, perhaps, hardware at the nanotechnology level, embedded into everything, that supports computational intelligence and its advances.

   Rather than the sky, the intelligence seems to be the limit.

   1.1. [Level 3] Write a comprehensive report on the future of computational intelligence.

2. With the growing availability and popularity of opinion-rich resources such as online review sites with multimodal data (numbers, characters, images, audio, and video), as well as blogs, wikis, and mash-ups, new opportunities and challenges arise as both data scientists and businesses now actively use computational intelligence tools to seek out and understand the opinions of others.

   One crucial challenge for the innovative businesses is to be able to harvest relevant information, and subsequently knowledge, from this overwhelming amount of multimodal data. Multimodal sentiment analysis can benefit from computational intelligence approaches that could provide models that integrate quantitative, textual, audio, and visual features to discover sentiment.

   Innovative businesses are constantly looking for new products and services. Car manufactures know the lessons of the product life cycle well. The availability and popularity of online review sites, with multimodal data, allows car companies to quickly and inexpensively get consumers' reaction to the concept of a proposed new product. Consumer expectations and preferences for alternative fuels, including hydrogen, are high on the list for the car manufacturers. Hydrogen has been touted as an alternative to petrol, provided there is a safe, fast way to store it onboard a vehicle.

2.1. [Level 3] Conduct research and write a comprehensive report on the current state of the use of computational intelligence in multimodal sentiment analysis.

2.2. [Level 4] Propose a research project for your Ph.D. dissertation that will support the construction and deployment of a sophisticated, computational intelligence tool to capture the six Ekman emotions (anger, disgust, fear, joy, sadness, surprise) and their polarity orientations (positive, negative) from online review sites with multimodal data (numbers, characters, images, audio, and video) for hydrogen-fueled cars.

3. Personal health messages, augmented with images and video, captured through inter-patient communications within online communities represent an innovative path toward providing updates about consumer-derived health status. Computational intelligence tools seem to be a natural fit for capturing and processing personal health messages from online blog, wiki, and mash-up boards. The approach could be used to demonstrate the ability to track trends in consumers' positive or negative opinion (sentiment) regarding particular drugs over time. Such analysis could down the road serve as a tool for identifying possible adverse drug reactions.

3.1. [Level 1] Conduct a literature review of applications of computational intelligence used for inter-patient communications within online communities.

3.2. [Level 2] Compare different sentiment-harvesting strategies, and provide recommendations for their possible augmentation.

3.3. [Level 3] For your graduate thesis work, use these findings to correlate significant changes in sentiment to U.S. Food and Drug Administration (FDA) cautionary announcements and warnings.

Bibliography

Adamo, J. M., "Fuzzy Decision Tree," *Fuzzy Sets and Systems*, Vol. 4, pp. 207–219, 1980.

Anderson, C., "The end of theory: The data deluge makes the scientific method obsolete," *Wired 16*, p. 7, 2008.

Anderson, J. A., "Cognitive and Psychological Computation with Neural Models," *IEEE Transactions on Systems, Man, and Cybernetics*, Vol. 13, pp. 799–815, 1983.

Baas, S. M. and Kwakernaak, H., "Rating and Ranking of Multiple-Aspect Alternatives Using Fuzzy Sets," *Automatica*, Vol. 13, pp. 47–58, 1977.

Bagher-Ebadian H., Soltanian-Zadeh, H., Setayeshi, S., and Smith, S. T., "Neural network and fuzzy clustering approach for automatic diagnosis of coronary artery disease in nuclear medicine," *IEEE Transactions on Nuclear Science*, Vol. 51, Issue 1, pp. 184–192, 2004.

Baldwin, J. F. and Guild, N. C. F., "Comparison of Fuzzy Sets on the Same Decision Space," *Fuzzy Sets and Systems*, Vol. 2, pp. 213–231, 1979.

Ballato, J., Theoretical Performance of Polymer Optical Fibers, NTC grant M01-CL01, 2001.

Bandler, W. and Kohout, L., "Fuzzy Relational Products and Fuzzy Implication Operators," Report #FRP 1, Dept. of Mathematics, University of Essex, 1978.

Bezdek, J. C., *Pattern Recognition with Fuzzy Objective Function Algorithms*, Plenum Press, New York, 1981.

Bichsel, M. and Seitz, P., "Minimum Class Entropy: A Maximum Information Approach To Layered Networks," *Neural Networks*, Vol. 2, pp. 133–141, 1989.

Bohachevsky, I. O., Johnson, M. E., and Stein, M. L., "Generalized simulated annealing for function optimization," *Technometrics*, Vol. 28, pp. 209–217, 1986.

Bortolan, G. and Degani, R., "A Review of Some Methods for Ranking Fuzzy Subsets," *Fuzzy Sets and Systems*, Vol. 15, pp. 1–19, 1985.

Buckley, J. J., Hayashi, Y., and Czogala, E., "On the Equivalence of Neural Networks and Fuzzy Expert Systems," in: Proceedings of International Joint Conference on Neural Networks, Baltimore, Vol. 2, pp. 691–695, 1992.

Camacho-Zuniga, C. and Ruiz-Trevino, F., A New Group Contribution Scheme to Estimate the Glass Transition Temperature for Polymers and Diluents, *Ind. Eng. Chem. Res.* Vol. 42, pp. 1530–1534, 2003.

Cartwright, H. M., Applications of Artificial Intelligence in Chemistry, Oxford: Oxford Univ. Press, Oxford, U.K., 1994.

Chen, S. H., "Ranking Fuzzy Numbers with Maximizing Set and Minimizing Set," *Fuzzy Sets and Systems*, Vol. 17, pp. 113–129, 1985.

Chen, S., Cowan, C. F. N., and Grant, P. M., "Orthogonal Least Squares Learning Algorithm for Radial Basis Function Networks," *IEEE Transactions on Neural Networks*, Vol. 2, No. 2, pp. 302–309, 1991.

Chen, X., Sztandera, L. M., and Cartwright, H. M., "A Neural Network Approach to the Prediction of Glass Transition Temperature of Polymers," *International Journal of Intelligent Systems* 23(1), pp. 22–32, 2008.

Chen X., Sztandera, L. M., Cartwright, H. M., and Granger-Bevan, S., "The Use of Computational Intelligence in the Design of Polymers and in Property Prediction," 7th International Conference on Bio-Inspired Models of Network, Information, and Computing Systems, Lugano, 2012.

Chow, L. R. and Chang, W., "A New Ranking Technique of Fuzzy Alternatives and Its Applications to Decision Making," *Policy and Information*, pp. 31–48, 1983.

Cios, K. J., Goodenday, L. S., and Wedding, D. K. II, "A Bayesian Approach for Dealing With Uncertainties in Detection of Coronary Artery Stenosis Using a Knowledge-Based System," *IEEE Engineering in Medicine and Biology*, pp. 53–58, 1989.

Cios, K. J., Freasier, R. E., Goodenday, L.S., and Andrews, L. T., "An Expert System for Diagnosis of Coronary Artery Stenosis Based on T1-201 Scintigrams Using the Dempster-Shafer Theory of Evidence," *CABIOS*, Oxford University Press, Vol. 6, No. 4, pp. 333–342, 1990.

Cios K. J. and Moraes I., "ALFS: An Inductive Learning Algorithm," *Kybernetes*, MCB University Press, Vol. 20, No. 3, pp. 19–30, 1991.

Cios, K. J. and Liu, N., "A Comparative Study of Machine Learning Algorithms for Generation of a Neural Network Architecture," in: *Artificial Neural Networks*, T. Kohonen, et. al. Eds., Elsevier Science Publishers B. V. (North Holland), Vol. 1, pp. 189–194, 1991.

Cios, K. J. and Sztandera, L. M., "Generation of Fuzzy Sets and Expert Rules for Diagnosis of Heart Disease," in: Proceedings of International AMSE Conference on Signals and Systems, Warsaw, Vol. 1, pp. 37–44, 1991.

Cios, K. J. and Sztandera, L. M., "Generation of Fuzzy Sets and Expert Rules for Diagnosis of Heart Disease," in: Proceedings of the 4th International Symposium on Fuzzy Systems and Signals, Warsaw, pp. 101–108, 1991.

Cios, K. J., Shin, I., and Goodenday, L., "Using Fuzzy Sets to Diagnose Artery Coronary Stenosis," *IEEE Computer Magazine*, Vol. 24, No. 3, pp. 57–63, 1991.

Cios, K. J. and Liu, N., "A Machine Learning Method for Generation of a Neural Network Architecture: A Continuous ID3 Algorithm," *IEEE Transactions on Neural Networks*, Vol. 3, No. 2, pp. 280–291, 1992.

Cios, K. J. and Sztandera, L. M., "Continuous ID3 Algorithm with Fuzzy Entropy Measures," in: Proceedings of the 1st International Conference on Fuzzy Systems and Neural Networks, San Diego, pp. 469–476, 1992.

Cios, K. J., Sztandera, L. M., Vary, A., and Baaklini, G. Y., "Prediction of Flexural Strength and Density of Silicon Nitride in Structural Ceramics Using Fuzzy Set Theory," Technical Manuscript, NASA-Lewis Research Center, TM-106049, 1993.

Cios, K. J., Baaklini, G. Y., Vary, A., and Tjia, R., "Radial Basis Function Network Learns Ceramic Processing and Predicts Related Strength and Density," Technical Manuscript, NASA-Lewis Research Center, TM-106048, 1993.

Cios, K. J., Baaklini, G. Y., Vary, A., and Sztandera, L. M., "Fuzzy sets in the prediction of flexural strength and density of silicon nitride ceramics." *Materials Evaluation*, Vol. 52, Issue 5, pp. 600–606, 1994.

Cios, K. J., Goodenday, L. S., and Sztandera, L. M., "Hybrid intelligence system for diagnosing coronary stenosis." *IEEE Engineering in Medicine and Biology Magazine* (special issue on Applications of Fuzzy Logic), Vol. 13, Issue 5, pp. 723–729, 1994.

Cios, K. J. and Liu, N., "A machine Learning algorithm using integer linear programming," *Kybernetes*, MCB University Press, U.K. 1994.

Cios, K. J. and Sztandera, L. M., "Ontogenic Neuro-Fuzzy Algorithm—FCID3," *Neurocomputing*, Vol. 14, pp. 383–402, 1997.

Curteanu S. and Cartwright H. M., "Neural Networks Applied in Chemistry. I. Determination of the Optimal Topology of Multilayer Perceptron Neural Networks." *Journal of Chemometrics*, Vol. 25, pp. 527–549, 2011.

Cybenko, G., "Approximation by Superposition of a Sigmoidal Function," *Mathematics of Control, Signals, and Systems*, Vol. 2, pp. 303–314, 1989.

De Luca, A. and Termini, S., "A Definition of a Nonprobabilistic Entropy in the Setting of Fuzzy Sets Theory," *Information and Control*, Vol. 20, pp. 301–312, 1972.

De Luca, A. and Termini, S., "Entropy of L-Fuzzy Sets," *Information and Control*, Vol. 24, pp. 55–73, 1974.

De Luca, A. and Termini, S., "On the Convergence of Entropy Measures of a Fuzzy Set," *Kybernetes*, Vol. 6, pp. 219–227, 1977.

Delgado, M., Verdegay, J. L., and Vila, M. A., "On Valuation and Optimization Problems in Fuzzy Graphs (A General Approach and Some Particular Cases)," *ORSA Journal of Computation*, Vol. 2, pp. 74–83, 1990.

Dombi, J., "A General Class of Fuzzy Operators, the De Morgan Class of Fuzzy Operators and Fuzziness Measures," *Fuzzy Sets and Systems*, Vol. 8, pp. 149–163, 1982.

Dubois, D. and Prade, H., *Fuzzy Sets and Systems: Theory and Applications*, Academic Press, New York, 1980.

Dubois, D. and Prade, H., "Ranking Fuzzy Numbers in the Setting of Possibility Theory," *Information Sciences*, Vol. 30, pp. 183–224, 1983.

Dubois, D. and Prade, H., "A Review of Fuzzy Set Aggregation Connectives," *Information Sciences*, Vol. 36, pp. 85–121, 1985.

Elter, M., Schulz-Wendtland, R., and Wittenberg, T., "The prediction of breast cancer biopsy outcomes using two CAD approaches that both emphasize an intelligible decision process," *Medical Physics*, 34(11), pp. 4164–4172, 2007.

Emptoz, H., "Nonprobabilistic Entropies and Indetermination Measures in the Setting of Fuzzy Sets Theory," *Fuzzy Sets and Systems*, Vol. 5, pp. 307–317, 1981.

Fahlman, S. E. and Labiere, C., "The Cascade-Correlation Learning Architecture," Technical Report CMU-CS-90-100, Department of Computer Science, Carnegie Mellon University, 1990.

Fisher, R. A., "The Use of Multiple Measurements in Taxonomic Problems," *Ann. Eugenics*, Vol. 7, pp. 179–188, 1936.

Frank, C., Garg, A., Sztandera, L. M., and Raheja, A., "Forecasting Women's Apparel Sales using Mathematical Modeling," *International Journal of Clothing Science and Technology*, Vol. 15, Issue 2, pp. 107–125, 2003.

Fujitsu: Ghost Miner, http://www.fqs.pl/business_intelligence/products/ghostminer, 2014.

Fukuda, J., "Reliability, Excel, Kettelle's Algorithm, and Inventory of Repairable Spare Parts," February, 2008.

Gaines, B. R., "Foundations of Fuzzy Reasoning," *International Journal of Man-Machine Studies*, Vol. 8, pp. 623–668, 1976.

Galushkin, A. I., "Neural Networks Theory," Springer, New York, 2007.

Gibson, G. and Schroeder, B., "Computer Failure Data Repository (CFDR)," http://cfdr.usenix.org/, 2009.

Gupta, M. M. and Qi, J., "On Fuzzy Neuron Models," in: *Fuzzy Logic for the Management of Uncertainty*, L. A. Zadeh and J. Kacprzyk, Eds., John Wiley & Sons, Inc., New York, pp. 479–491, 1992.

Harris, J., *An Introduction to Fuzzy Logic Applications*, Kluwer, Dordrecht, 2000.

Hayashi, Y., Czogala, E., and Buckley, J. J., "Fuzzy Neural Controller," in: Proceedings of the 1st International Conference on Fuzzy Systems and Neural Networks, San Diego, pp. 197–202, 1992.

Hayashi, Y., Buckley, J. J., and Czogala, E., "Fuzzy Expert Systems Versus Neural Networks," in: Proceedings of International Joint Conference on Neural Networks, Baltimore, Vol. 2, pp. 720–726, 1992.

Hayashi, Y., Buckley, J. J., and Czogala, E., "Fuzzy Neural Network with Fuzzy Signals and Weights," in: Proceedings of International Joint Conference on Neural Networks, Baltimore, Vol. 2, pp. 696–701, 1992.

Higashi, M. and Klir, G. J., "On Measures of Fuzziness and Fuzzy Complements," *International Journal of General Systems*, Vol. 8, pp. 169–180, 1982.

Hinton, G. E. and Sejnowski, T. J., "Learning and Relearning in Boltzman Machines," in: *Parallel Distributed Processing*, D. E. Rumelhart and J. L. McClelland, Eds., Vol. 1, Cambridge, MA, MIT Press, pp. 282–317, 1986.

Hirota, K. and Pedrycz, W., "Fuzzy Logic Neural Networks: Design and Computations," in: Proceedings of the IJCNN'91 (2), Singapore, pp. 1588–1593, 1991.

Hornik, K., Stinchcombe, M., and White, H., "Multilayer Feedforward Networks are Universal Approximators," *Neural Networks*, Vol. 2, pp. 359–366, 1989.

Hornik, K., "Approximation Capabilities of Multilayer Feedforward Networks," *Neural Networks*, Vol. 4, pp. 251–257, 1991.

Hougen, D. R. and Omohundro, S. M., "Fast Texture Recognition Using Information Trees," Technical Report, Department of Computer Science, University of Illinois at Urbana-Champaign, 1988.

Ishibuchi, H., Fujioka, R., and Tanaka, H., "Possibility and Necessity Pattern Classification Using Neural Networks," *Fuzzy Sets and Systems*, Vol. 48, pp. 331–340, 1992.

Ishibuchi, H., Fujioka, R., and Tanaka, H., "Neural Networks that Learn from Fuzzy If-Then Rules," *IEEE Transactions on Fuzzy Systems, Vol.* 1, No. 2, pp. 85–97, 1993.

Iwamoto, M., Hahimoto, K., Inaba, M., Kobayashi, T., Hattori, M., and Komatsu, O., "Application of Fuzzy Control for Iron Ore Sintering Process," *Transaction of Iron and Steel Institute of Japan (ISIJ)*, Vol. 28, pp. 341–345, 1988.

Jain, R., "A Procedure for Multiple-Aspect Decision Making Using Fuzzy Sets," *International Journal of System Science*, Vol. 8, pp. 1–7, 1977.

Kandel, A., *Fuzzy Techniques in Pattern Recognition*, Wiley, New York, 1982.

Kandel, A., *Fuzzy Mathematical Techniques with Applications*, Addison-Wesley Publishing Company, Reading, MA, 1986.

Katritzky, A. R., "Quantitative Structure-Property Relationship (QSPR) Correlation of Glass Transition Temperatures of High Molecular Weight Polymers." *J. Chem. Inf. Model*, Vol. 38, pp. 300–304, 1998.

Kaufmann, A., *Introduction to the Theory of Fuzzy Subsets*, Academic Press, New York, 1975.

Keller, J. M., Gray, M. R., and Givens, J. A., Jr., "A Fuzzy K-nearest Neighbor Algorithm," *IEEE Transactions on Systems, Man, and Cybernetics*, Vol. 15, No. 4, pp. 580–585, 1985.

Keller, J. M. and Hunt, D. J., "Incorporating Fuzzy Membership Functions Into the Perceptron Algorithm," *IEEE Transactions on Pattern Analysis and Machine Intelligence*, Vol. 7, No. 6, pp. 693–699, 1985.

Keller, J. M. and Yan, B., "Possibility Expectation and Its Decision Making Algorithm," in: Proceedings of the 1st International Conference on Fuzzy Systems and Neural Networks, San Diego, pp. 661–668, 1992.

Keller, J. M., Yager, R. R., and Tahani, H., "Neural Network Implementation of Fuzzy Logic," *Fuzzy Sets and Systems*, Vol. 45, pp. 1–12, 1992.

Keller, J. M. and Tahani, H., "Backpropagation Neural Networks for Fuzzy Logic," *Information Sciences*, Vol. 62, pp. 205–221, 1992.

Kerre, E. E., "The Use of Fuzzy Set Theory in Electrocardiological Diagnostics," in: *Approximate Reasoning in Decision Analysis*, M. M. Gupta and E. Sanches, Eds., North-Holland, Amsterdam, pp. 277–282, 1982.

Khashman, A., "Credit risk evaluation using neural networks: Emotional versus conventional models," *Applied Soft Computing*, Vol. 11, Issue 8, pp. 5477–5484, 2011.

Klir, G. J. and Folger, T. A., *Fuzzy Sets, Uncertainty and Information*, Prentice Hall, 1988.

Knopfmacher, J., "On Measures of Fuzziness," *J. Math. Anal. and Appl.*, Vol. 49, pp. 529–534, 1975.

Koczy, L. T., "Fuzzy Graphs in the Evaluation and Optimization of Networks," *Fuzzy Sets and Systems*, Vol. 46, pp. 307–319, 1992.

Kosko, B., "Fuzzy Entropy and Conditioning," *Information Sciences*, Vol. 40, pp. 165–174, 1986.

Kosko, B., *Neural Networks and Fuzzy Systems*, Prentice Hall, Englewood Cliffs, 1992.

Lang, K. and Witbrok, M. J., "Learning to Tell Two Spirals Apart," in: *Proc. of 1988 Connectionist Models Summer School*, Touretzky, Hinton, Sejnowski, Eds., Morgan-Kaufmann, pp. 52–59, 1988.

Li, R. J. and Lee, E. S., "Ranking Fuzzy Numbers—A Comparison," in: Proceedings of the North American Fuzzy Information Processing Society, NAFIPS'87, pp. 169–204, 1987.

Li, X., Huang, M. C., Shen, K., and Chu, L., "An Empirical Study of Memory Hardware Errors in a Server Farm," HOTDEP Workshop, 2007.

Licata, G., "Employing fuzzy logic in the diagnosis of a clinical case," *Health*, Vol. 2, No. 3, pp. 211–224, 2010.

Loo, S. G., "Measures of Fuzziness," *Cybernetica*, Vol. 20, pp. 201–210, 1977.

Lutz, W. E., "The Ready Application of Neural Networks," Proceedings of the 40th Conference of the Urban and Regional Information Systems Association, pp. 649–654, 2002.

Malek, J., Sebri, A., Mabrouk, S., Torki, K., and Tourki, R., "Automated Breast Cancer Diagnosis Based on GVF-Snake Segmentation, Wavelet Features Extraction and Fuzzy Classification," *Journal of Signal Processing Systems*, Kluwer Academic Publishers, Volume 55, Issue 1–3, pp. 49–66, 2009.

Mangasarian, O. and Wolberg, W., "Cancer diagnosis via linear programming," *SIAM News*, Vol. 23, No. 5, pp. 1–18, 1990.

Marrero, J. and Gani, R., "Group-contribution based estimation of pure component properties," *Fluid Phase Equilibria*, pp. 183–208, 2001.

McCahon, C. and Lee, E. S., "Comparing Fuzzy Numbers: The Proportion of the Optimum Method," *International Journal of Approximate Reasoning*, Vol. 4, pp. 159–181, 1990.

McCulloch, W. and Pitts, W., "A Logical Calculus of the Ideas Immanent in Nervous Activity," *Bulletin of Mathematical Biophysics*, Vol. 5, pp. 115–133, 1943.

McEntire, B. J., Taglialavore, A. P., Heichel, D. N., Bright, E., Yeckley, R. L., Holowczak, J. E., and Quackenbush, C. L., "Silicon Nitride Component Development for Advanced Gas Turbine Engines," in: Proceedings of the 27th Automotive Technology Development Contractors Coordination Meeting, Society of Automotive Engineers, Inc., Warrendale, PA, pp. 341–349, 1990.

Mitsumoto, M., "Some Methods of Fuzzy Reasoning," in: *Advances in Fuzzy Set Theory*, M. M. Gupta, R. K. Regade, and R. R. Yager, Eds., North Holland, Amsterdam, pp. 117–136, 1979.

Mitsumoto, M. and Zimmermann, H. J., "Comparison of Fuzzy Reasoning Methods," *Fuzzy Sets and Systems*, Vol. 8, pp. 253–285, 1992.

Moody, J. and Darken, C., "Fast Learning in Networks of Locally Tuned Processing Units," *Neural Computing*, Vol. 1, No. 2, pp. 281–294, 1989.

Murakami, S., Maeda, H., and Immamura, S., "Fuzzy Decision Analysis on the Development of Centralized Regional Energy Control System," in: Preprints of IFAC Conference on Fuzzy Information, Knowledge Representation and Decision Analysis, pp. 353–358, 1983.

Nakamura, K., "Preference Relations on a Set of Fuzzy Utilities as a Basis for Decision Making," *Fuzzy Sets and Systems*, Vol. 20, pp. 147–162, 1986.

Neural Technologies, Minotaur, http://www.neuralt.com/our_technology.html, 2014.

Nguyen, D. and Widrow, B., "The Truck Backer-Upper: An Example of Self-Learning in Neural Networks," in: Proceedings of International Joint Conference on Neural Networks (IJCNN-89), Vol. II, pp. 357–363, 1989.

Novak, V., *Fuzzy Sets and Their Applications*, Adam Higler, Bristol, England, 1989.

Omohundro, S. M., "Efficient Algorithm With Neural Network Behavior," *Complex Systems*, Vol. 5, pp. 348–350, 1987.

Pedrycz, W., *Fuzzy Control and Fuzzy Systems*, John Wiley & Sons, 1989.

Pedrycz, W., "Neurocomputations in Relational Systems," *IEEE Transactions on Pattern Analysis and Machine Intelligence*, Vol. 13, No. 3, pp. 289–297, 1991.

Quinlan, J. R., "Induction of Decision Trees," *Machine Learning*, Vol. 1, pp. 81–106, 1986.

Rosenfeld, A., "Fuzzy Graphs," in: *Fuzzy Sets and Their Applications to Cognitive and Decision Processes*, L. A. Zadeh, K. S. Fu, K. Tanaka, and M. Shimura, Eds., Academic Press, New York, pp. 77–97, 1975.

Rumelhart, D. E., Hinton, G. E., and Williams, R. J., "Learning Internal Representations by Error Propagation," in: *Parallel Distributed Processing*, D. E. Rumelhart and J. L. McClelland, Eds., MIT Press, Cambridge, MA, pp. 318–362, 1986.

Safian, R., "The World's Most Innovative Companies 2014," *Fast Company*, Issue 183, March 2014.

Sanders, W. A. and Baaklini, G. Y., "Correlation of Processing and Sintering Variables with the Strength and Radiagraphy of Silicon Nitride," *Ceramic Engineering and Science Proceedings*, Vol. 7, pp. 839–859, 1986.

Sanford, J. and Sztandera, L. M., "Classification Data Mining Using Fuzzy Logic," Conference Proceedings of the International Academy of Business and Public Administration Disciplines, New Orleans, 2010, pp. 120–127, 2010.

Sanford, J. and Sztandera, L. M., "Classification data mining with hybrid fuzzy logic aggregation," *WSEAS Transactions on Computers*, Vol. 10, Issue 11, pp. 379–389, 2011.

Schmitz, H. J., Poppel, G., Wunsch, F., and Krey, U., "Fast Recognition of Real Objects by an Optimized Hetero-Associative Neural Network," *Journal of Physics*, Vol. 51, pp. 167–183, 1990.

Schmuller, J., "Three Faces of Fuzziness, Theory, Practice, and Applications," *PC AI Fuzzy Logic and Neural Networks*, Vol. 7, No. 2, pp. 14–15, 26–29, 1993.

Schroeder, B. and Gibson, G., "Disk Failures in the Real World," in Proceedings of FAST'07, 5th USENIX Conference on File and Storage Technologies, San Jose, CA, pp. 1–16, 2007.

Sembi, B. S. and Mamdani, E. H., "On the Nature of Implication in Fuzzy Logic," in: Proceedings of the 9th International Symposium on Multiple Valued Logic, pp. 143–151, 1979.

Shannon, C. E., "The Mathematical Theory of Communication," *The Bell System Technical Journal*, Vol. 27, pp. 379–423, 623–656, 1948.

Sirat, J. A. and Nadal, J. P., "Neural Trees: a New Tool For Classification," *Network*, Vol. 1, pp. 423–438, 1990.

Sztandera, L. M., "Aspects of Microprocessor Control in the X-ray Industrial System," in: Proceedings of the 3rd International Conference on Signal Transformation, Bydgoszcz, pp. 289–294, 1988.

Sztandera, L. M., "Expert Controller in the X-ray Industrial System," in: Proceedings of the 3rd International Workshop on Process Automation, Wroclaw, Vol. 3, pp. 73–76, 1988.

Sztandera, L. M., "Experience Augmented Expert System in Process Automation," in: Proceedings of International Conference "Control and Optimization of Transport and Industrial Processes," Zakopane, pp. 381–390, 1988.

Sztandera, L. M. and Stachowicz, M. S., "A Fuzzy Model of the Video Process," in: Preprints of the 2nd Joint IFSA-EC EURO-WG Workshop "Progress in Fuzzy Sets in Europe," Vienna, pp. 176–177, 1988.

Sztandera, L. M. and Stachowicz, M. S., "A Fuzzy Luminance Process," *AMSE Review*, AMSE Press, Vol. 10, No. 2, pp. 41–45, 1989.

Sztandera, L. M., "Experience Augmented Linguistic Model for a Real Industrial System," *Advances in Modeling and Simulation*, Vol. 19, No. 3, pp. 55–63, 1990.

Sztandera, L. M., "Relative Position Among Fuzzy Subsets of an Image," M. S. Thesis, University of Missouri-Columbia, Columbia, MO, 1990.

Sztandera, L. M. and Keller, J. M., "Spatial Relations Among Fuzzy Subsets of an Image," in: Proceedings of the 1st International Symposium on Uncertainty Modeling and Analysis, Queens Park, IEEE Computer Society Press, pp. 207–211, 1990.

Sztandera, L. M. and Cios, K. J., "A Method for Defining a Relative Position of Fuzzy Sets," in: Proceedings of International AMSE Conference on Signals and Systems, Warsaw, Vol. 1, pp. 45–54, 1991.

Sztandera, L. M. and Cios, K. J., "A Method for Defining a Relative Position of Fuzzy Sets," in: Proceedings of the 4th International Symposium on Fuzzy Systems and Signals, Warsaw, pp. 39–48, 1991.

Sztandera, L. M. and Cios, K. J., "Decision Making in Fuzzy Environment Generated by a Neural Network Architecture," in: Proceedings of the 5th IFSA World Congress, Seoul, Vol. 1, pp. 73–76, 1993.

Sztandera, L. M., "Fuzzy Sets in Self-Generating Neural Network Architectures," Ph.D. Dissertation, University of Toledo, Toledo, OH, 1993.

Sztandera, L. M., Goodenday, L. S., and Cios K. J., A Neuro-Fuzzy Algorithm for Diagnosis of Coronary Artery Stenosis, *Computers in Biology and Medicine Journal*, 26(2), pp. 97–107, 1996.

Sztandera, L. M., "Identification of the Most Significant Properties Influencing Tactile Fabric Comfort Using Regression Analysis," WSEAS Transactions on Computers, Vol. 2(8), pp. 302–311, 2009.

Sztandera, L. M., "Optimal Inventory of Computer Repair Parts—A Fuzzy Systems Approach," in: Proceedings of PRDC'10, Tokyo, Japan, pp. 225–226, 2010.

Sztandera, L. M., "Spare Parts Allocation—Fuzzy Systems Approach," in: Proceedings of the 15th WSEAS International Conference on Computers, Corfu, Greece, pp. 245–249, 2011.

Szu, H. and Hartley, R., "Fast Simulated Annealing," *Phys. Lett. A*, Vol. 122, No. 8, pp. 157–162, 1987.

Takahashi, Y.," A fuzzy Query Language for Relational Databases," in: *Fuzziness in Database Management Systems*, Physica Publisher, Heidelberg, pp. 365–384, 1995.

Trillas, E. and Riera, T., "Entropies of Finite Fuzzy Sets," *Information Sciences*, Vol. 15, pp. 159–168, 1978.

Tsukamoto, Y., Nikiforuk P. M., and Gupta M. M., "On the Comparison of Fuzzy Sets Using Fuzzy Chopping," in: Proceedings of the 8th Triennial IFAC World Congress, 5, pp. 46–52, 1981.

Van Krevelen, D., *Properties of Polymers*, Elsevier Science Publishing Company, New York, 1990.

Wang, L. X., "Fuzzy Systems are Universal Approximators," in: Proceedings of the 1st IEEE International Conference on Fuzzy Systems, San Diego, pp. 1163–1170, 1992.

Wang, L. X. and Mendel, J., "Generating Fuzzy Rules by Learning from Examples," *IEEE Transactions on Systems, Man, and Cybernetics*, Vol. 22, No. 6, pp. 1414–1427, 1992.

Wasserman, P. D., "Combined Back-propagation Cauchy Machine," in: Proceedings of International Neural Network Society, 1988.

Watkins, R. C., Reynolds, K. M., DeMara, R. F., Georgiopoulos, M., Gonzalez, A. J., and Eaglin, R., "Exploring Data Mining Technologies as Tools to Investigate Money Laundering," *Journal of Policing Practice and Research*, Vol. 4, No. 2, pp. 163–178, 2003.

Watson, S. R., Weiss, J. J., and Donnell, M. L., "Fuzzy Decision Analysis," *IEEE Transactions on Systems, Man, and Cybernetics*, Vol. 9, pp. 1–9, 1979.

Wolberg, W. and Mangasarian, O., "Multisurface method of pattern separation for medical diagnosis applied to breast cytology," Proceedings of the National Academy of Sciences, Vol. 87, pp. 9193–9196, 1990.

XLBIT, Genetic algorithm for Microsoft Excel, http://www.xlpert.com, 2010.

XL-Miner, Excel add-in developed by Cytel Software Corporation and distributed by Resampling Stats, Inc., http://www.resample.com, 2010.

Yager, R. R., "On the Measure of Fuzziness and Negation. Part I: Membership in the Unit Interval," *International Journal of General Systems*, Vol. 5, pp. 221–229, 1979.

Yager, R. R., "On the Measure of Fuzziness and Negation. Part II: Lattices," *Information and Control*, Vol. 44, pp. 236–260, 1980.

Yager, R. R., "On Choosing Between Fuzzy Subsets," *Kybernetes*, Vol. 9, pp. 151–154, 1980.

Yager, R. R., "A Procedure for Ordering Fuzzy Subsets Over the Unit Interval," *Information Sciences*, Vol. 24, pp. 143–161, 1981.

Yager, R. R., "Fuzzy Prediction Based on Regression Models," *Information Sciences*, Vol. 26, pp. 45–63, 1982.

Yager, R. R., "On the Implication Operator in Fuzzy Logic," *Information Sciences*, Vol. 31, pp. 141–164, 1983.

Yager, R. R., Ochvinnikov S., Tong R. M., and Nguyen H. T., *Fuzzy Sets and Applications*, John Wiley and Sons, New York, 1987.

Yager, R. R., "On Ordered Weighted Averaging Aggregation Operators in Multicriteria Decision Making," *IEEE Transactions on Systems, Man, and Cybernetics*, Vol. 18, No. 1, pp. 183–190, 1988.

Yager, R. R., "Modeling and Formulating Fuzzy Knowledge Bases Using Neural Networks," Technical Report MII-1111, Machine Intelligence Institute, Iona College, 1991.

Yager, R. R., "Implementing Fuzzy Logic Controllers using a Neural Network Framework," *Fuzzy Sets and Systems*, Vol. 48, pp. 53–64, 1992.

Zadeh, L. A., "Fuzzy Sets," *Information and Control*, Vol. 8, pp. 338–353, 1965.

Zadeh, L. A., "A Fuzzy Set Theoretic Interpretation of Linguistic Hedges," *Journal of Cybernetics*, Vol. 2, pp. 4–34, 1972.

Zadeh, L. A., "Outline of a New Approach to the Analysis of Complex Systems and Decision Processes," *IEEE Transactions on Systems, Man, and Cybernetics*, Vol. 3, pp. 28–44, 1973.

Zadeh, L. A., "The Concept of a Linguistic Variable and its Application in Approximate Reasoning, Part I, II, and III," *Information Sciences*, Vol. 8, pp. 199–249; Vol. 8, pp. 301–357; Vol. 9, pp. 43–80, 1975.

Zadeh, L. A., "Calculus of Fuzzy Restriction," in: *Fuzzy Sets and Their Applications to Cognitive and Decision Processes*, L. A. Zadeh, K. S. Fu, K. Tanaka, and M. Shimura, Eds., Academic Press, New York, pp. 1–39, 1975.

Zadeh, L. A., "A Theory of Approximate Reasoning," *Machine Intelligence*, Vol. 9, J. E. Hayes, D. Michie, and L. I. Mikulich, Eds., John Wiley, New York, pp. 149–194, 1979.

Zadeh, L. A., "Possibility Theory and Soft Data Analysis," *Mathematical Frontiers of Social and Policy Sciences*, L. Cobb and R. M. Thrall, Eds., Westviero Press, Boulder, pp. 69–129, 1981.

Zadeh, L., "A Computational Approach to Fuzzy Quantifiers in Natural Languages," *Comput. Math. Appl.*, Vol. 9, pp. 149–184, 1983.

Zadeh, L., "The Role of Fuzzy Logic in the Management of Uncertainty in Expert Systems," *Fuzzy Sets and Systems*, Vol. 11, pp. 199–227, 1983.

Zadeh, L. A., "Interpolative Reasoning in Fuzzy Logic and Neural Networks Theory," Plenary talk given at the 1st IEEE International Conference on Fuzzy Systems FUZZ-IEEE, San Diego, 1992.

Zahirniak, D. R., Chapman, R., Rogers, S. K., Sutter, B. W., Kabrisky, M., and Pyati, V., "Pattern Recognition Using Radial Basis Function Networks," in: Proceedings of the Conference on Aerospace Applications of AI, Dayton, pp. 1–12, 1990.

Zimmermann, H. J., *Fuzzy Sets, Decision Making and Expert Systems*, Kluwer Academic Publishers, Boston, MA, 1987.

Zimmermann, H. J., *Fuzzy Set Theory and its Applications*, 2nd revised edition, Kluwer Nijhoff Publishing, Boston, MA, 1991.

Index

A

B

C

D

E

F

G

H

P

Q-R

S

T

U-V

W-X-Y-Z